RELEVANCE

RELEVANCE

■

**Making
Stuff That
Matters**

TIM MANNERS

Portfolio

PORTFOLIO

Published by the Penguin Group

Penguin Group (USA) Inc., 375 Hudson Street, New York, New York 10014, U.S.A. · Penguin Group (Canada), 90 Eglinton Avenue East, Suite 700, Toronto, Ontario, Canada M4P 2Y3 (a division of Pearson Penguin Canada Inc.) · Penguin Books Ltd, 80 Strand, London WC2R 0RL, England · Penguin Ireland, 25 St. Stephen's Green, Dublin 2, Ireland (a division of Penguin Books Ltd) · Penguin Books Australia Ltd, 250 Camberwell Road, Camberwell, Victoria 3124, Australia (a division of Pearson Australia Group Pty Ltd) · Penguin Books India Pvt Ltd, 11 Community Centre, Panchsheel Park, New Delhi – 110 017, India · Penguin Group (NZ), 67 Apollo Drive, Rosedale, North Shore 0632, New Zealand (a division of Pearson New Zealand Ltd) · Penguin Books (South Africa) (Pty) Ltd, 24 Sturdee Avenue, Rosebank, Johannesburg 2196, South Africa

Penguin Books Ltd, Registered Offices:
80 Strand, London WC2R 0RL, England

First published in 2008 by Portfolio,
a member of Penguin Group (USA) Inc.

10 9 8 7 6 5 4 3 2 1

LIBRARY OF CONGRESS CATALOGING IN PUBLICATION DATA

Manners, Tim.
  Relevance : making stuff that matters / by Tim Manners.
    p. cm.
  Includes index.
  ISBN 978-1-59184-220-0
  1. Brand name products.   2. Branding (Marketing)   I. Title.
  HD69.B7 M36 2008
  658.8'27—dc22   2008024947

Printed in the United States of America
Designed by Chris Welch · Set in Minion

Contents

As long as I have strawberries, I feel prosperous.

—DAVID X MANNERS

(1912–2007)

Introduction

An epidemic of irrelevance has brought once-powerful brands to their knees. The virus is an inordinate fixation on demographics-driven strategies, fashion-forward images, and media-focused communications.

The autopsy points to a lack of organic growth.

The cure is a reaffirmation of the essence of marketing, which is simply to help people solve problems and live happier lives. Interestingly, at least a few brands have managed to make comebacks after years in the wilderness.

- Levi's reasserted relevance when it created wardrobe solutions for men.

- Hasbro reasserted relevance when it reinvented board games for today's time-pressed consumers.
- Staples reasserted relevance when it stopped wasting its shoppers' time with extraneous products.

If these brands can rediscover their relevance, so can your brands. The cure, however, requires overturning certain precepts that have shaped marketing's "best practices" for the last fifty years or more.

- **Demographics Are Dead.** You can't get from good to great by marketing solely on the basis of consumer age, gender, or ethnicity. Relevant brands take on and solve problems that transcend traditional demographic boundaries.
- **Fashion Is Passé.** It is no longer sustainable to create products or services that are vulnerable to the vagaries of consumer aspirations, fashions, or fads. Brands that depend too heavily on buzz for growth are not built to last.
- **Advertising Smells Funny.** Advertising might not be dead yet, but it is sickly, and new media can be just as frail as old media. Whether online, offline, or grapevine, advertised messages are irrelevant most of the time for most brands.

The answer is to design meaningful solutions and provide them when and where consumers need them most. That answer may not be as glamorous as a television commercial or as hip as a TXT MSG, but it will create growth because it is accountable to the happiness of the people who would buy your brands.

Relevant brands understand certain principles:

- *Insight.* Relevant brands care about what we actually do, not just what we think.
- *Innovation.* Relevant brands know the difference between what is purely remarkable and what actually works.
- *Investment.* Relevant brands understand the imperative of sparing no expense when it comes to satisfying our needs.
- *Design.* Relevant brands live and breathe simplicity.
- *Experience.* Relevant brands realize that it is more important to touch us in real life than on television.
- *Value.* Relevant brands are more than worth every penny.

Relevance is divided into three parts. The first part defines the problems facing irrelevant brands, part two outlines solutions, and part three describes what success looks like for relevant brands.

The book is laced with case study examples of 87 brands as well as insights provided via interviews with 50 top marketing executives from America's top corporations.

Each example is capped with key take-away points, providing a roadmap to relevance and a pathway to sustainable growth for years to come.

PART I

■

Relevant Problems

CHAPTER 1

Demographics

Marketing, Not Apartheid

> Demographics matter less and less—not just to
> marketers, but to everybody.
> —MIKE LINTON

When I asked Mike Linton a series of questions about how he goes about targeting consumers by age, gender, and ethnicity, he didn't take the bait. At the time, Mike was chief marketing officer of Best Buy (he is now chief marketing officer of eBay). He didn't deny that Best Buy sometimes ran some ads along ethnic lines, but he also said the segmentation was more about consumer behavior than ethnicity or any other demographic pigeonholes. "We don't talk about individual segments," he said, explaining that the best approach was to customize each store so that it is more attractive to *anyone* who is likely to shop there.

It was a surprising response from the chief marketing officer of a company that had made splashy news about segmenting its shoppers based, at least in part, on their demographic profiles. But it echoed what I had been hearing from other top marketers from some of America's most respected companies.

Leslie Kilgore, chief marketing officer of Netflix, told me that her brand didn't profile or target consumers, that it simply offered a great movie-watching experience—a proposition that knows no demographic boundaries.

Anne Saunders, a former senior vice president of marketing of Starbucks (currently with Bank of America), pointed out that the Starbucks experience is pretty much the same for everyone regardless of their age, income, or ethnicity. She said Starbucks' success was mainly due to its rather universal appeal as a coffeehouse.

John Fleming, chief merchandising officer of Wal-Mart, agreed when I suggested that demographics, as a tool of the marketing trade, were not as relevant as they used to be. He said, "Thirty or forty years ago it was very different. Back then, people in different economic zones had different expectations, but that's not really the case anymore. Everybody has access to all the same information, and basically everybody wants it all—whatever the hot new product is, everybody wants it, and they're going to figure out a way to pay for it."

Costco's marketing chief, Paul Latham, told me that while there is "a demographic profile of a Costco member that is more affluent, more college educated, higher in home ownership, with generally more kids living at home," he doesn't spend a lot of time analyzing Costco shoppers. He added, "Costco has a tremendous amount of information on each of our members, but to be honest, we don't use a lot of it. The bulk of what we do for our members is done pretty much across the board. All of our coupon programs and internal marketing efforts are pretty much targeted at all of our existing members. . . . We certainly use our member information to help us model for prospective members, but to a large degree we rely on our intuition."

Perhaps most direct of all was Jim Adams, executive director of marketing for Chipotle Mexican Grill. When I asked Jim whether he targeted any particular demographic, he replied, "Yes—people who eat!"

Jim said that Chipotle instead takes aim at a certain kind of personality. That personality is the type of person "who is concerned about what goes into his or her body, who is looking for superior quality, who wants to go into a cool atmosphere. . . . We're looking for someone who is not just a price-driven consumer. We're looking for a quality-driven consumer."

Are Demographics Discredited?

I put the question of whether demographics were discredited as a means of targeting consumer segments to executives from some pretty successful companies. Their responses were remarkably consistent.

Larry Flanagan, MasterCard

Demographics are not discredited, but often they are less effective versus behavioral and attitudinal insights. We really focus on looking at the motivation of what really drives behavior as well as understanding transactional behavior.

Cindy Hennessy, Cadbury-Schweppes

The consumption behavior across demographics actually is very pronounced in the beverage category. If you look at per capita consumption by age and type of beverage consumption by age there are some very definitive segmentations.

But as any category matures, demographics must be married with other types of segmentation. Most of that segmentation is psychographic or behavioral. For example, salads simply never sold at a fast-food restaurant in any volume until the last five years, and I think it's because of the aging of the population. People are now trying to undo the damage they've done with their bad eating habits over the years and are now trying to strike a balance.

Ruby Anik, formerly of Best Buy (currently of J. C. Penney)

Demographics are a really good start, but we prefer to go deeper. Just because people live in the same neighborhood or have reached the same stage in life does not necessarily mean they think the same way or want the same things.

We've really moved to attitudinal and behavioral segmentation. That's what our one-to-one loyalty-marketing program is based on. We mine the customer insights based on their needs states and what they've purchased. We don't want you to just buy a box from us. We want to figure out how we can create a whole experience for you.

Spencer Hapoienu, Insight Out of Chaos
I think demographics are becoming more and more discredited. If you think about how everyone uses all the media and how quickly you can change your lifestyle or behavior because of new technology, it renders demographics less and less relevant. For example, YouTube is changing the behavior of lots of different kinds of consumers. We may be talking about a relatively small segment of the population overall, but it is probably a very wide range of demographics that watches YouTube. So I don't know how you can look only at demographics and say, "That's our user base" anymore.

It is safe to say, then, that at least seven of America's smartest marketers have disabused themselves of the idea that consumers can be fully understood as discrete little pockets of men, women, and children; households earning more or less than $100,000; black, white, or otherwise.

It is not that such profiling isn't sometimes useful or even successful. And it is not as though any of these companies do not engage in it at some level. It is that too often such typecasting is substituted for real understanding about what makes us, the consumers, tick.

The result is that brands frequently sell themselves short by failing to see their consumers as we see ourselves. More often than not we are more similar than we are different from one another when it comes to what we expect from our brands.

Amazing Met

Before Peter Gelb came along, revenues at the New York Metropolitan Opera "had been flat for six straight years, more tickets were being sold at discount to fill the house, and the average age of the audience had jumped to 65," reported Stephanie Clifford in *Inc.* magazine.

Peter started by "fixing" the product—"enlisting filmmaker Anthony Minghella . . . to stage Puccini's *Madama Butterfly*." But his goal, he said, was not "to suddenly turn the Met into an audience of twenty-year-olds, but to draw upon the broader cultural audience of New York City" and "engage the public in new ways.

"The model for me is professional baseball and football," continued Peter, "where the more connected they are electronically, the more people want to come and experience the real thing." For example, he made available free tickets to the show's final dress rehearsal. He also simulcast the show's opening performance in Times Square, setting up seats right on the sidewalk.

The bottom line was that revenues for the 2006 season increased by "more than \$8 million . . . and the overall audience expanded 15 percent." Advance sales for the next season were up by 10 percent.

■ **The Metropolitan Opera didn't just generate buzz and awareness; it succeeded by communicating that the Met was for everyone.**

Wicked Tweens

The Broadway success of *Wicked* sent other producers scrambling to attract the "tween" demographic, but their scramble was problematic, reported Campbell Robertson in the *New York Times*. The problem was that even though "teenage and tween girls are the demographic of the moment" on Broadway and can create the buzz that makes a hit, they can't carry a show's success by themselves. *Wicked* worked because it was "created for a general audience" while also "attracting a fanatical, often face-painted following of teenagers and tweens."

By comparison, *Legally Blonde*, which was also strongly appealing to teen and tween girls, had a much rougher go of it because just about nobody else seemed to care. That included moms: "This is a little more for *them*," said Tacey Carroll, who attended a performance of *Legally Blonde* only because her daughter, Jamie, needed a chaperone.

The show's producers had calculated that *Legally Blonde*

would work on Broadway mainly because of its $96 million success as a major motion picture. What they didn't count on, apparently, was that movies are a lot cheaper to produce than Broadway shows, and tickets are a lot cheaper, too.

- **Where a niche audience could create a Hollywood hit, it took a broader cross-section of consumers to see success on Broadway.**

The Great White Way

Conventional wisdom has it that to succeed on Broadway with a musical, you need to attract just one kind of consumer: white middle-aged women. The producers of *The Color Purple* totally blew that particular bit of marketing dogma to pieces, according to an article in the *Wall Street Journal* by Brookes Barnes.

Brookes began by noting that shows featuring African-American characters—such as *Dreamgirls* and *The Wiz*—traditionally play to audiences that are only about 25 percent black. Overall, less than 4 percent of all Broadway show ticket buyers are black. Apparently, they don't call it the Great White Way for nothing.

The Color Purple didn't buy into that kind of prejudice. The marketing strategy combined an ad campaign that conveyed "movement and happiness" with a media strategy that targeted "smaller neighborhood publications and newsletters" that normally didn't advertise Broadway shows.

The show's Web site was redesigned to raise the comfort level of tourists by including hotel packages and tips on how to get around Manhattan.

Ticket prices were lowered to entice first-timers to take a chance on a Broadway experience. The result was that *The Color Purple* played to audiences who were "over 50 percent black, with some performances in the 80 percent range."

■ **Everything *The Color Purple* did to build a black audience almost certainly would work as well with other audiences—and other shows that don't necessarily feature black themes or talent.**

Books for Blacks

For the last twenty years or more, the business of marketing has turned itself inside out over the issue of "integrated marketing." That discussion is all about the challenges of making the various marketing disciplines work together in perfect harmony.

Twenty years later most marketers have still not quite gotten to the bottom of integrated marketing. That so much time and energy have been spent on the topic is more sad than tragic, given that the very concept of "marketing" is premised on the integration of its many disciplines: advertising, promotion, public relations, and so forth. The term *integrated marketing* is redundant.

The industry's time might have been better spent discussing *segregated marketing*, or the practice of separating one consumer segment from another in the marketplace. Nowhere is this practice more flagrant than in the retailing of books, where "blacks-only" departments have been the norm at major chains including Borders and Waldenbooks, as reported by Jeffrey Trachtenberg in the *Wall Street Journal*. Barnes & Noble, however, has not segregated books by authors based on their race.

This issue is more relevant than ever because African Americans are spending about twice as much on books today as they did ten years ago. Both memberships and sales for the Black Expressions book club grew by double digits at a time when overall bookstore sales were falling.

Surprisingly, some prominent African-American authors have not been totally enraged about this retail segregation. Brandon Massey, who writes in what otherwise might be classified as the "horror" genre, said he realized that merchandising his books in a blacks-only section of the store helped his base find his books. But he also said he understood that the practice probably limited his sales, too.

No sales data exist that support which approach sells more books, but as Mr. Massey observed, "Most nonblack readers aren't going to go to the African-American section."

■ **A good book is a good book, and its relevance is based on the content of its pages, not the color of its author.**

Whyville, Toyota

"A lot of what we do is based on the mind-set rather than the specific age group," said Deborah Senior, a marketing manager, explaining to Julie Bosman of the *New York Times* why the Toyota Scion paid for product placement on Whyville.net, an online community for kids.

Other car marketers have used product placement in video and online games to attract customers. Cadillac, for example, placed itself in a Microsoft Xbox 360 game. But Toyota was among the first to apply the idea that maybe it makes sense for a car company to target kids. That is not only because young kids represent an outsized influence on their parents but also because they might grow up with a certain loyalty to Toyota based on fond childhood memories created online at Whyville.net.

Matthew Diamond of Alloy Media and Marketing thinks it is probably money well spent: "You're establishing that brand presence and positive association, since important buying decisions are forthcoming," he said.

■ **By recognizing that kids are just as interested in cars as anyone, Toyota got a head start on establishing its relevance for years to come.**

Cool for Kids

When Reveries.com surveyed 254 senior-level marketers and asked about the potential of "adult" brands to be marketed to children, a surprisingly large number—67 percent—said the potential was anywhere from good to excellent. It was surprising mainly because one would have expected more of the marketers to express concern about the potential ethical or moral issues of marketing to kids in certain categories. Then again, we're talking about the marketing business here!

In follow-up interviews, I asked folks from Cadbury Adams, LEGO Systems, Nintendo, and GoldnFish Marketing about which traditional "adult" categories had the most potential for growth by marketing to kids.

Bill Higgins, Cadbury Adams

There is a growing trend among kids to have an interest in badge-value electronic devices—spurred on by the iPod. The potential for other technology like BlackBerry, for example, may be limited because of the costs involved. However, for kids, instant messaging, instant communications—maybe BlackBerry could take that and shift it.

Chuck McLeish, LEGO

Financial services are an opportunity. Kids really are not taught some of the fundamentals of saving, building wealth, how to spend money, balance a checkbook, and think about longer-range goals. It is not the most interesting thing to a kid, but it would be a tremendous service if that could be done.

Perrin Kaplan, Nintendo

Health clubs, perhaps. There should be a place that serves those who have the paunch in the middle and those who will get the paunch in twenty years. South Beach should not be just for older people.

Steve Gold, GoldnFish

The PGA—I've never understood, when there are so many kids who golf in this country, that there has never been an effort to make golfing go younger. I'm curious from the sport's perspective why that is, why they've never even made an attempt at creating a kids' circuit of events or somehow making it more entertaining.

Let 'em Eat Grapes

Marketing's cloistered view of kids as just another demographic group isn't just a missed opportunity; it's a disservice to kids. The reason is that most marketing to kids centers on the food and beverage category. On any given day an Internet search of the term *kids marketing* is dominated by links to Web sites and news stories about children and obesity. That is just so sad and so revealing about where marketing's energies tend to focus.

One would hope that *kids marketing* would turn up all kinds of cool campaigns that actually help kids lead better lives somehow. Not a chance.

You can accuse me of not looking hard enough, but in the more than nine years that I've scoured daily newspapers and other periodicals in search of what is innovative or merely interesting in marketing, I can only remember finding one news article about a major marketing campaign that truly took kids' health to heart. That was a 2006 story by Tara Parker-Pope in the *Wall Street Journal*.

It was about a campaign called Verb, which was designed to get kids to exercise. Part of the campaign involved television commercials, but its centerpiece was half a million 6-inch yellow rubber balls imprinted with the word VERB and distributed to kids, primarily via schools and camps. The kids were supposed to play with the ball, blog about the experience, and then give the ball to a friend. According to the *Journal*, a follow-up "study of more than 2,700 schoolkids . . . showed that 9- and 10-year-old kids who had seen the Verb campaign reported one-third more physical activity during their free time than kids who hadn't seen Verb."

Verb was as imaginative as it was effective, so much so that it earned Arc Worldwide, the agency behind it, an award at the prestigious Cannes Lions International Advertising Festival.

Unfortunately, instead of more campaigns like Verb, we have more and more of the usual run of stories about kids and the obesity epidemic. For example, topping a search of kids marketing stories was an article in the *Wall Street Journal* about a research study by the University of Liverpool that suggested a rather strong connection between what kids watched on television and what they ate as a result.

The study was of two groups of kids, ages five to eleven, who watched ten ads followed by a cartoon. One group saw ads for toys, while the other group saw ads for food. The kids were then offered a spread of snacks, ranging from healthy to junky. The five- to seven-year-olds who saw the food ads ate "14 percent to 17 percent more calories" than the kids who saw the toy ads. Among nine- to eleven-year-olds, the caloric intake was "84 percent to 134 percent higher." Naturally, the overweight kids ate more of the "sugary, high-fat foods." The only good news here, according to the report, was that "kids' consumption of healthy foods, such as grapes . . . also jumped after seeing food ads."

Whether this study can be considered conclusive is debatable, but its findings certainly seem obvious and predictable. Advertising is supposed to motivate consumption, after all, and it is always comforting to see advertising work as advertised!

However, despite advertising's apparent effectiveness among kids in this study, no reasonable person could blame advertisers for single-handedly turning our kids into "plumpkins." That would be untrue. The obesity problem is much more complicated than that. But wouldn't it be great if the brightest minds in the marketing business applied more of their creative talents to solving the childhood obesity problem than they do to contributing to it?

A big part of the problem is that we, as adults, tend to under-estimate kids (actually we, as marketers, tend to underestimate people in general). But the Verb campaign shows that kids are, in fact, eager to have fun with a ball if we encourage that. The Liverpool study suggested that kids would just as soon eat grapes if that is what they were offered.

In fact, there was a great story in the *New York Times* about a guy named Timothy Cipriano who runs the cafeteria at Bloom-field High School in Connecticut. His coworkers were aston-ished when Timothy unloaded "several bushels of fresh Connecticut corn." They thought he had misplaced his mind. They were used to working with the kind of corn that came in cans. They didn't think the kids would touch corn with a husk on it. But guess what?

"We steamed it and put it out there," said Timothy. "The kids shucked it themselves and went crazy for it. We ran out halfway through the first shift." Witness the power of not un-derestimating kids.

Gay Cars

As Alex Williams wrote in the *New York Times*, "Cars are no more straight or gay than cellphones, office chairs or weed whackers," but that hasn't stopped perceptions that certain cars can be statements about a driver's sexual orientation.

Such perceptions tend to swirl most often around the new

VW Beetle, the Mini Cooper, the Mazda MX-5 Miata, and, of course, the Subaru Outback (known among some drivers as the Lesbaru). Of those cars, only Subaru has made an overt effort to appeal to gay drivers, having run an ad campaign starring Martina Navratilova and the slogan, "It's not a choice. It's the way we're built." Ramone Johnson, a gay journalist, actually compiles a list of "Top 10 Gay Cars," and Gizmodo, the gadget blog, ran results of a reader poll on the most gay automobiles.

Some gay consumers are understandably incensed by such surveys. "We're really polling people's prejudices here," said one respondent to the Gizmodo poll. But others, such as Judith Halberstam, proudly drove a black Mazda 3 hatchback that she said was "butch." She commented, "If you are a masculine woman, you might not feel bad about it, so you might become excited about knowing how to fix your pickup or driving a '68 Mustang."

Meanwhile, Frank Markus of *Motor Trend* magazine observed that cars favored by gay consumers were often a function of the fact that they usually didn't have kids. That meant they tended to buy more expensive and less practical cars. In other words, gay consumers can be a highly attractive segment for car marketers.

Adam Bernard of General Motors said the company pursued the gay marketplace without regard for any potential fallout among other consumers. "Frankly, the money's all the same color," he said. In fact, according to data compiled by Gaywheels.com, the most frequently researched cars are the

Toyota Yaris ($12,000), "followed by the Toyota Camry, which was the No. 3–selling car in America" in 2006.

■ **When it comes to buying cars, the similarities between gay and straight consumers are bigger than the differences.**

Brokeback Strategy

Brokeback Mountain, the famous movie about gay cowboys, was one of the most profitable and most praised in 2006, but it owed much of its success to women and straight men. According to a *Wall Street Journal* article by John Lippman, the film's distributor, Focus Features, pursued a marketing strategy that was deliberately designed to avoid having the film tagged as an art-house film for gays. Appealing to women was key to the strategy. Movie posters emphasized that the movie was a love story of sorts, while the movie's trailers emphasized the happier sides of the relationships between the cowboys and their wives. The trailers also were paired with films with plenty of female appeal, such as Jodie Foster's *Flightplan*.

The proof of the strategy's effectiveness was evident in the way the film's audience composition shifted over time. On the first weekend the audience was indeed 60–40 gay males. However, over the next three weeks the split flipped to 60–40 females. After *Brokeback Mountain* won at the Golden Globes, straight men started to buy tickets, and women accounted for about 55 percent of the total.

Before long, *Brokeback* was doing well in theaters nationwide, including in America's heartland where one chain reported that *Brokeback* was beating the film *Munich* by three to one. "I wouldn't say people are not seeing it because of its homosexual content," said Debby Brehn of Douglas Theatres in Lincoln, Nebraska.

- **Emphasizing its relevance to audiences beyond its base enabled *Brokeback Mountain* to catapult itself from "an art-house movie for gays" to a mainstream blockbuster hit.**

American Women

American Airlines hit some serious turbulence when it "started a Web site just for its female travelers," according to Joe Sharkey, writing in the *New York Times*. American said it was just trying to demonstrate its "continued commitment to the women's market," but apparently many women weren't exactly impressed.

"There are so many things that are infuriating about this lip-service nonsense that I can't begin to list them all," said Julie Pfeffer, a frequent flier. "Why does AA feel that female travelers need things explained to them that male travelers don't? Are we that dumb?"

As one flier put it, "I'm quite indignant that AA thinks this kind of silly fluff is going to appeal to me. I want a clean plane, a comfortable seat, and good service at a fair price. . . . That's what my husband wants. That's what my colleagues of both genders want. . . . Instead, they offer us dirty planes, wretched seats, and increasingly awful service—sometimes at reasonable prices, sometimes not—and wholly silly programs like this one."

Another angry customer suggested AA should get its employees to treat passengers better and "have someone who understands the human spine . . . design their seats."

■ **Hopefully, American Airlines learned that stereotyping its customers is worse than being irrelevant. It is insulting.**

Speed of Song

In the short time it was around, Delta's Song Airlines was often criticized for being a pale imitation of JetBlue. Less well known was that every little thing Song did to please its passengers went back to a very simple insight: that women are the gatekeepers of air travel decisions and that airlines all but ignore them.

As Tim Mapes, the airline's chief marketing officer, explained in a 2004 interview with Reveries.com: "We decided to let every other airline talk to the 48 percent of the U.S. population that is male and be the one airline that is positioning itself to better meet the needs of the other 52 percent of the population."

So, did that mean Song was a "women's airline"? Tim Mapes said that it did not. "The economics of the business simply just don't allow that," he said. "What was interesting was that by building an airline designed to meet the needs of women, we met the needs of just about everyone else."

■ **Song may have failed as an airline, but Tim Mapes deserved credit for understanding the difference between targeting a consumer segment and creating a relevant brand experience.**

Relevant brands often find their focus within a key demographic group but do not shape their strategies purely on issues of age, gender, ethnicity, or income. Sometimes the result is surprising, but, more important, it is also a growth driver for the brand.

When he was chief marketing officer of Dunkin' Donuts, John Gilbert told me that Hispanics were a key source of growth for the brand, but there was a twist: "The insight is that most U.S. Hispanic consumers would like to have the product for which a brand is best known. So for Dunkin' Donuts it's donuts and coffee; Hispanics don't want us serving flan. However, it isn't a stretch to believe that Hispanic products for general-market consumers could be a reasonable product for us at some point."

In other words, Hispanic consumers want what is non-Hispanic, and the non-Hispanics want what's Hispanic! What matters here is that Dunkin' Donuts, if it applied its insights carefully, would be more relevant to more people all around. That would give it an even stronger platform for growth.

Rick Ridgeway, Patagonia's president of communications, expressed a similar reluctance to put too much stock in demographics-only approaches: "Patagonia is not a very demographically constrained brand. Our apparel doesn't seem to have any negative connotations for young people just because older people wear it. When we dig into why, it goes back to Patagonia's core values, which seem to be values that cut across generational lines."

- **Relevant brands are focused on achieving growth by basing their strategies on relatively simple insights that are far more universal than a demographics-only perspective could ever be.**

CHAPTER 2

Aspirations

The Happiness Factor

We hold these truths to be self-evident, that all men are created equal, that they are endowed by their Creator with certain unalienable Rights, that among these are Life, Liberty, and the pursuit of Happiness.

—Thomas Jefferson

That line, written by Jefferson for the Declaration of Independence, is arguably the most "American" sentence ever written. Sure, he snitched most of it from an Englishman, John Locke, but Jefferson tweaked it, more or less changing the last word from "Property" to "Happiness." And it is that last word—Happiness (with a capital "H")—that so perfectly captures the most American of ideals.

Jefferson is remembered for many things. Marketing is not one of them, but it should be. The Declaration of Independence was not only a "killer" positioning statement but its incredibly complicated and extraordinarily dangerous proposition (a new nation based on an experimental model) all but hung on a single word. Okay, *three* words. But "Happiness" is the key word, the ultimate call to action. If they had bumper stickers back then, you can be sure the "smiley face" would have been invented much earlier. ☺

Think about the most successful brands in recent memory. It isn't hard; it is actually getting to be a rather predictable list. What is it that Apple, Starbucks, JetBlue, and Trader Joe's promise? It's the pursuit of Happiness. Why is the list so short? Because most of what passes for marketing today (and yesterday, for that matter) isn't about Happiness at all. In fact, it's sheer Misery.

It is bad jingles, intrusive telemarketers, junk mail, and those little cards that fall out of magazines. It is most television and radio commercials, pop-up ads on the Internet, and cashiers who ask us if we want one of their blasted loyalty cards.

It is as if Jefferson never changed the word "Property" to "Happiness." When most people think of marketing, they think of anything but Happiness. Try to find a little Happiness by escaping to the movies, and what do you find? More ads—before the movie, embedded in the movie, and after the movie. You want a coupon with that? No? Can we have your ZIP code then?

Philips Simplicity

A grand total of one advertiser, Philips Electronics, seems to understand what really makes us happy. Philips wanted to buy all the available ad time at movie theaters in Minneapolis and Boston and take credit for not using it to advertise its products.

They thought it would be cool to give us a little break and simply run a short message letting us know that they were sponsoring the cinema silence—a moment of Happiness, if you will. Unfortunately, Screenvision, the company that sold the screen time at the theaters, thought that Philips was making a mockery of movie theater ads and nixed the idea.

Philips has succeeded elsewhere, however. At a cost of $2 million, it sponsored an entire episode of CBS's *60 Minutes*. But instead of using its media buy to run its ads, Philips donated the minutes back to the viewers so that they could enjoy longer news segments. More recently, Philips sponsored a cut in the commercial time on NBC's *Nightly News with Brian Williams*, from seven minutes to just one minute. According to an article by Karlene Lukovitz in the *New York Times*, it paid off for them: The newscast "saw an eight percent ratings lift and generated 9,400 grateful e-mail messages over three days."

The significance of this strategy by Philips Electronics, which the brand aptly called its "sense and simplicity" campaign, was all the more striking because Philips is in a category, consumer electronics, that is almost always marketed as cool, trendy, and "must have." As Eric Plaskonos of Philips explained in the *Times*, the Philips strategy is instead premised on reducing the amount of clutter in people's lives rather than just pitching their products.

■ **The nexus of happiness and relevance is easily located by brands like Philips that realize their marketing strategy is about *our* lives and not just *their* products.**

The Compact

Marketers also tend to confuse happiness with materialism. That is not very surprising since practically the entire advertising industry is built on the premise that we can *buy* our way into being smarter, sexier, cooler, or more popular. Deep down we all know this is one big lie. We have known that money can't buy us love ever since the Beatles told us so back in 1964. Most of those in the advertising business also know better than to believe their own hype, although they remain quite sure that we will believe it.

Maybe advertising's basic premise was true in its heyday, back in the 1950s and 1960s, but it is not true anymore and is just not relevant.

Some folks were so unhappy with marketing that they formed a club of sorts called the Compact. It is named after the Mayflower Compact, which was the Pilgrims' pledge to pursue a higher purpose when they first arrived at Plymouth Rock in 1620. In the modern-day version, the pledge is simply not to buy anything new other than food, medicine, and other essentials.

The idea was to find Happiness through Simplicity, and it is a reaction to consumerism, which members of the Compact thought was out of control. An overwhelming majority of Americans agree with them, apparently. As reported by Elizabeth Weise in *USA Today*, a survey by sociologist Juliet Schor of Boston College found that "81 percent of Americans say the country is too focused on shopping and spending, and 88 percent think it is too materialistic."

James Roberts, a Baylor University marketing professor, said all that consumerism is a pursuit of something other than Happiness. "The research is overwhelmingly clear," he said. "The more materialistic you are, the less happy you are. We get Happiness through the love of others and sense of community. But we've been told by Madison Avenue that Happiness can come through the mall."

■ **The advertising industry's assumption that appealing to a consumer's aspirations is the key to marketing success still holds true, but those aspirations can be less materialistic than they used to be.**

Rodeo Retail

Putting shoppers at ease and in a mood to buy is especially tough for luxury retailers on Rodeo Drive, and many of them fail miserably, reported Christina Binkley in the *Wall Street Journal*. "Rodeo sends messages that are not welcoming," admitted Wes Carroll of Chopard, a watch and jewelry retailer, which seems to do a better job than most.

This is the challenge: "There's a fine line between positioning themselves as lofty—to signal just the right amount of exclusivity—and being so haughty they alienate their customers."

Chopard manages, in part, by stocking "lollipops and coloring books to occupy the kids while parents gawk at million-dollar pendants."

But at Van Cleef & Arpels the prevailing attitude can be contemptuous, delivered by a "saleswoman's frown and a suspicious 'Can I help you?'" At least that's what Christina got when she tried shopping there with Dan Hill, "a specialist in emotion."

Actually, Dan thought that a certain level of contempt was not a bad thing but that it should be limited to window displays, not the way shoppers are treated once they are inside the store. A little contempt can be effective in a display, he said, because it communicates "superiority." But when directed at a shopper, "it's devastating." That kind of contempt, said Dan, is generally communicated via a clerk's body language—specifically the mouth. It's not what the clerk says, though.

According to Dan, "Only seven percent of communication relies on verbal exchange." It's what's going on at the corners of the clerk's mouth. Simply put: Is the clerk smiling or not? Is one corner of the mouth raised but not the other? And it's not enough just to smile once. The smile must be repeated and with as much conviction as possible.

The winning retailer, based on Christina and Dan's store checks, was Coach. And it wasn't just that the clerk was smiling. It was also the "bright, cheery" ambiance and that the clerks weren't all "model-thin." The emotional effect was almost enough for Christina to spring for a $495 pair of boots. When she didn't, the clerk slipped her a business card—and smiled.

■ **If you want to make your customers happy, it helps to
remember to smile. And smile again. And smile again.**

Levi's Revival

Apple probably gets the credit (or blame) for reinventing a
features-and-benefits business as a fashion business. Levi's may
get the credit for reinventing the fashion business as a features-
and-benefits business with its Dockers line of apparel.

Dockers looked dead, pretty much, when John Goodman
arrived at Levi's as president of the Dockers brand. But just a
few years later the khakis were back, thanks to a so-called lifestyle marketing strategy that was not so much about stoking
aspirations as it was about solving problems.

It's not that Dockers was totally giving up on being fashionable. As John Goodman explained to Ray A. Smith in the *Wall
Street Journal*, "I'm a merchant, a product guy through and
through. . . . So it's been about making sure our product is the
best quality, the most relevant, and in most cases, the most
fashion-forward it can be."

Being fashionable is still important because we're talking
about apparel here, after all. But the relevance factor is more
about function than fashion and is largely a result of surround-
ing Dockers' khakis with a complete line of complementary
apparel. Even more to the point, Dockers aligned its line of mens-
wear to correspond to four occasions: work, weekend wear,

dressing up, and golf. In other words, Dockers reasserted its relevance by helping men, in particular, organize their wardrobes.

The Dockers brand had declined 21 percent in the fiscal year ending November 2004 but grew every quarter between late 2005 and early 2007.

Whether that wardrobe is upscale or trendy is irrelevant. Dockers achieved its success with the insight that there are plenty of people who just want to get dressed and get it over with. Most likely they are the same people who get their coffee at Dunkin' Donuts instead of Starbucks.

■ **For the Dockers man, happiness was never having to think twice about what to wear.**

Dunkin's Tribe

Before it got started on its expansion, Dunkin' Donuts made sure there were enough of its kind of coffee drinkers to support tripling the number of its stores. Dunkin' had already concluded that its customers were less "pretentious" than the typical Starbucks patron.

As reported by Janet Adamy in the *Wall Street Journal*, Dunkin's customers had quickly made it clear that they didn't like Dunkin's newly stylized coffee cups with a sleeker-looking logo. Nor did they care for the earth-toned decor of some of

Dunkin's newer stores. They were suspicious of those fancy latte machines, too.

So Dunkin' fielded some surveys with questions along the lines of whether a customer "sometimes had to use his or her looks to get ahead." To its delight Dunkin' found that about "one-third of the country is made up of people" who didn't identify with such behavior. Even better, a lot of them didn't live anywhere near a Dunkin' Donuts. And so the expansion was on—with the goal of taking Dunkin' from its starting point of about 5,300 stores to a total of about 15,000 over the next several years.

Dunkin' has also made its stores more "warm and welcoming," to encourage its laptopping customers to linger a bit longer, as they do at Starbucks. And as for those coffee cups, let's just say Dunkin' is back to chunky Styrofoam and its endearingly workaday pink and orange motif.

■ **After flirting with copying the style and flash of Starbucks, Dunkin' wisely chose to reaffirm the simple things that made its core customers happiest.**

Wal-Mart Style

Wal-Mart has grappled with a similar situation relative to its flashier rival, Target Corporation. Indeed, lots of people jumped

on Wal-Mart when it moved "upscale" in its apparel department. Of course, jumping on Wal-Mart has practically replaced baseball as the all-American pastime.

Wal-Mart's thinking actually wasn't all that bad. Wal-Mart's
John Fleming told me that the strategy was really about trying to
get its more fashion-conscious customers to shop in the apparel
department. As he saw it, there were plenty of Wal-Mart shoppers who were interested in finer styles and would buy them at
Wal-Mart if only they were available: "We simply want to make
sure that our offerings are relevant to a broader range of customers. The price points . . . aren't necessarily higher than other
items in the store. It's more that the styling is at a different level,
to make it more relevant to a different group of customers."

Please note his repeated use of the word *relevant*! Unfortunately, the idea may have been less successful than Wal-Mart
had hoped, perhaps because Wal-Mart has never been about
fashion. Its stock in trade has always been functionality.

■ **The concept of couture style ran counter to Wal-Mart's
core values, and it just didn't fly. It didn't make anyone
very happy.**

Penney Americans

J. C. Penney took its own special shot at Wal-Mart's attempts to
go upscale. Mike Ullman, J. C. Penney's CEO, was rather blunt

about it, actually. "We are *not* ashamed of Middle America," he said in an article by *USA Today*'s Mindy Fetterman. Describing his customers as women with "too little time, too little money, and two little kids," he blasted other retailers for "trying to drag Middle Americans upscale in one direction or downscale in another."

He added, "We don't think there's anything wrong with being 42 percent of American consumers." In other words, there's nothing wrong with going back to being what Penney's was before it tried to go upscale and lost $705 million in 2000, $928 million in 2003, and its stock was trading at $8.63 a share.

The simple shift back to what made its customers happy paid off for J. C. Penney. At this writing its stock is trading at $76.49.

■ **J. C. Penney succeeded where Wal-Mart stumbled simply by reaffirming its relevance to the everyday lives of its mainstream customers.**

A good chunk of the marketing community has become so caught up in "trading up" and "cheap chic" that it has forgotten high style isn't necessarily the same thing as high quality. It can't seem to remember that luxury is not defined by price. Luxury is defined by scarcity. Plenty of consumers are plenty happy just to be treated well and offered a good value. The experience may not be memorable for anything other than the elegance of its utility. These days that kind of experience is a rarity at any price.

Super 8 Motels

Reservations are not required at Super 8 Motels. In fact, about 65 percent of their customers just walk in and take a room at an average cost of about $50 a night.

It may not be the Marriott, where a full-service room goes for about $150 a night, and it certainly is not the Ritz-Carlton, where the average room costs around $290 a night. But according to an article by Jeff Bailey in the *New York Times*, Super 8 Motels promise clean rooms and friendly service, and they don't nickel-and-dime you for every little extra the way they do at the fancier hotels.

Where you might pay $10 or more a day for Internet service at a Marriott, every single one of the Super 8's 124,000 rooms has a free wireless connection. The chain also installed curved shower rods and upgraded mattresses and towels. Paul Pettit, who operates some forty Super 8 Motels across America, said the chain's simple touches pay for themselves in the form of repeat business.

■ **The best things in life may not always be free, but Super 8 Motels create happiness by not overcharging guests for the things that really matter.**

Happy Warriors

When I asked John Riordon, a former vice president of marketing for Virgin Atlantic Airways, what made his airline different from the rest, this is what he said:

> *It's the people, to be honest with you. We have an excellent group of people working in our marketing organization throughout the world. If you get the right people motivated in the right way, and you have a brand that people believe in, then you don't have an issue.*
>
> *One of our company foundations is that if we have a place where people enjoy working, that will be passed on to the customers who will see that and will enjoy flying with us and who will fly more often, which will give us more profit.*
>
> *So, as opposed to saying, "Let's first and foremost try to deliver shareholder value," we try to deliver employee value, which will deliver passenger value, which will deliver shareholder value. We're simply inverting the typical business model.*

Jack Kennard, senior vice president and director of global marketing services for Brown-Forman Beverages, added that there's a faulty assumption that marketers and salespeople are the only brand builders. He offered this advice on how to make certain that every employee helps ensure customer happiness:

Organize a small "battalion" of brand ambassadors for one brand rather than trying to educate every employee on all brands. Do that through corporate universities, Web sites, and electronically signing up memberships.

Then it's incumbent on brand teams to dedicate some resources to the care and feeding of employees and to treat them as champions—recognize them, reward them, let them know things that other people don't know.

Orientation of new employees should be heavily skewed toward what the company makes and why it is good. There is way too much HR in orientation and way too little brand building. They have the hat on backwards.

L. L. Bean There

The doors have no locks at L. L. Bean's flagship store in Freeport, Maine, because the store never closes. And the store never closes so that its customers can return anything they want, anytime they want.

"There is a satisfaction in knowing that Papa Bean is always there, arms open and waiting for you to return the blucher mocs you wore in prep school for a full refund," wrote Alex Kuczynski in the *New York Times*.

"L. L. Bean is . . . like the genial grandfather who is always up, reading by the fire, waiting to hear your questions or read you a story if you can't sleep." So committed is L. L. Bean to its open-door policy that it will even take back items that it says it will not—specifically, monogrammed goods: "L.L. Bean informs its customers that monogrammed items are not returnable, but customers do return these things every day, and the company takes them back." L. L. Bean simply puts them on a shelf and sells them to folks who want to pay less for, say, bath towels and don't mind if someone else's name is on them.

■ **It's kind of hard to be unhappy with a retailer that never locks its doors and will take back whatever you bought from them whether you have a valid complaint or not.**

Hook, Line, and Happiness

I asked Steve Fuller, senior vice president of corporate marketing for L. L. Bean, for his views on the relationship between employees and customer happiness. He responded:

Our customers, both on the phone and in the stores, trust our employees implicitly. Management can find that a little frustrating at times. For example, suppose you're shopping for a particular kind of skis, but L. L. Bean is not the best place to buy them. Our reps will say so. Yes, we lose a sale on a pair of skis, but if we had made the sale, the customer would not have been happy.

Training is a huge part of that. The Web is a bit more challenging, however, because it's a low-service channel. If you have a question about a product, talking to a person— whether it's in person at a store or on the phone—is often the simplest solution. That may not be the lowest cost from the service perspective, but whatever makes the customer happiest and answers their questions the fastest is what works best.

The total of employee and customer happiness is, of course, loyalty for everyone involved. Without loyalty a brand isn't just irrelevant, it's toast. Think about the smell of burning toast. That is the smell of your brand without loyalty.

So how do you create the happiness that results in loyalty? I asked execs from L. L. Bean, Avis, The Kroger Company, Barnes & Noble, McDonald's, and Harrah's Entertainment.

Steve Fuller, L. L. Bean

At the risk of sounding simplistic, it really is a matter of un- derstanding what customers are looking for and giving it to them. Customers want to pay a fair price for a good product, and they want to be treated well. They are remarkably consis- tent about that. In our case, they are remarkably savvy. They know what a fair price is.

We decided the best way to do that was simply to put the price next to the product. Our customers understood without our having to explain anything. The fundamental principles of creating a good product at a fair price and treating customers well can't be understated.

Scott Deaver, Avis

Brands are made out of excellent consumer experiences, not out of marketing. Usually that means giving customers things they want when they want them. But it's really not the giving that matters, it's the relationship building that the giving implies. If you make the customer jump through three hoops to earn a reward, you have done nothing to build loyalty.

[Continue] to develop the product with an ear to the consumer to make sure you are adding things the consumers have been wishing for. Finally, you need a winning recovery process for when things go wrong. You have to identify the problem and turn it around quickly.

Ken Fenyo, Kroger

There are four areas that we spend a lot of time working through—what we call the four keys. They are the things we'd like our customers to say about us: Your people are great. Your prices are good. The shopping experience makes me want to return. I get what I want plus a little.

In addition, about 40 percent of all U.S. households have one of our shopper cards, and through that we collect a ton of data. Using insights from that data we have been able to build deep relationships with the customers we already have, as opposed to focusing on getting new customers. We have taken these insights and used them to create an increasingly relevant and differentiated shopping experience.

David Gitow, Barnes & Noble

The simplest and most basic way Barnes & Noble builds loyalty is by creating an outstanding store experience. We have a large selection, and the fundamental basics of retailing are done in an excellent way. That is also true of our online experience.

We have a loyalty program where you pay $25 and get 40 percent off on best sellers, 20 percent off hardcover books, and 10 percent off everything else. But the way we build loyalty is by treating our customers right. If you have a terrible store with a terrible experience, having a loyalty program won't make a difference.

Eric Leininger, McDonald's

Loyalty is explicitly part of the McDonald's mission. Consumer relevance is the essential starting point for building loyalty, so we invest in understanding our customers and our marketplace, and in anticipating the future.

Our menu teams have a robust pipeline of activity to be on the right pace with changing consumer tastes with new menu items. Increasingly, we are also building ease-of-use elements into the way we interact with customers, whether through cashless payments, twenty-four-hour operations, or double-lane drive-throughs.

David Norton, Harrah's

Loyalty is about understanding what the brand should mean and then delivering that at every opportunity. Then we layer on that with our Total Rewards loyalty program, which is our mechanism to truly build loyalty and preference for the customer across all our casino brands. Building up the Total Rewards brand has been critical to our success.

The Regginator

Like so many other business goals, converting employees into cheerful brand ambassadors starts at the top. It is curious how rarely this happens. How many CEOs have truly personified their brands? Sir Richard Branson, Steve Jobs, Hugh Hefner . . . it's a short list.

Even shorter is the list of chief marketing officers who fashion themselves as passionate brand advocates, as one of their own best fans. True, that might be because none of them last long enough in their jobs to develop that kind of perspective. At most companies the CMO is looked upon as the employment equivalent of a rounding error.

But that is no excuse. Reggie Fils-Aime, who joined Nintendo U.S. as its executive vice president of sales and marketing, has proven the power of one person to energize its customers. Unless you are an avid gamer, you may never have heard of Reggie Fils-Aime. But if you are a member of the brand cult known as Nintendo, Reggie is nothing less than a demigod.

"Reggie is the light of Nintendo, nay, the light for the world!" posted one such believer on an Internet bulletin board. Another wrote: "When Reggie walks, his massive footprints fill with beautiful flowers for the children to enjoy."

The enthusiasm doesn't stop with words. Reggie's fan club created rap songs about him, drew comic strips glorifying him, and, in perhaps the ultimate accolade, fashioned Reggie action heroes immortalizing him. To what does Reggie Fils-Aime, who less than a year before toiled in near obscurity as chief marketing officer of VH-1, owe such ardor?

It is actually rather simple: Reggie spoke up for Nintendo's customers, and he did so in no uncertain terms. He stood up at the video game industry's big show, the Electronic Entertainment Exposition, and this is how he introduced himself: "My name is Reggie. I'm about kickin' ass. I'm about takin' names. And we're about making games."

Some of us might not understand exactly what Reggie was talking about, but his meaning was crystal clear to Nintendo's gamers. As Reggie himself told me, "These fans—these kids— want to see Nintendo bringing back fantastic games and driving the industry and driving innovation the way the company has for years and years. So they were proud, they were happy for someone like me to come in and articulate a very aggressive attitude—and, frankly, have the games and the innovations to back it up."

If you were to ask just about any other top marketing officer whether speaking for the consumer is a key part of the job, it is a safe bet that 100 percent of them would say that it is. But how many actually articulate that as directly and powerfully—and as purposefully—as does Reggie Fils-Aime?

We understand that CMOs are busy people. Yes, most of them are very, very busy trying to find their seats at the table in the coveted C suite, right next to the CEO, the CFO, the CIO, the COO, the CCO, the CAO, the CTO, the CBO, the CLO, the CKO, and, last but not least, the CZO. Conventional wisdom has it that the CMOs will find a permanent place around the big table once they figure out how to calculate the return on the money they spend on their marketing programs. That is certainly important. Just ask the CFO.

But they might also give a little thought to whether ROI might start with speaking up for their customers. Just ask Reggie—who, by the way, is now president of Nintendo North America.

It is not just about what's trendy, fabulous, chic, luxurious, sexy, or cool. Yes, we are all interested in those things, but the business of marketing—as just about everyone knows—too often leans too heavily on irrelevant superficialities that really don't make us all that happy.

- **Relevant brands seek to help people live happier lives, but they do so by addressing everyday issues, not by pandering to fashionable aspirations.**

CHAPTER 3

Advertising ·

Accountable to Whom?

Advertising is a tax for having an
unremarkable product.
—ROBERT STEPHENS

The men wear white shirts and skinny black ties, while the women don skirts and black tights. For about $150 they will hop into a black-and-white VW Beetle and drive to your home to cure whatever ails your digital lifestyle.

They are called the Geek Squad, and they are part of Best Buy's grand plan to maintain its position as America's retailer of really cool stuff—that is, all things digital. The notion is that while many folks are drawn to gizmos and gadgets, few are capable of either wiring their toys themselves or maintaining their wiredness.

The Geek Squad solves that problem—and does so cheerfully. As Dori Molitor of WomanWise, an agency that specializes in marketing to women, noted in *The Hub* magazine, Robert

Stephens, founder of the Geek Squad, said his business model is simply to "just be nice and fix it."

"As a niche, that idea is huge," Dori wrote, "given that 29 percent of all callers reportedly swear at their customer service representative and 21 percent scream at them. It's probably safe to assume that a majority of Geek Squad customers escape their frustrations with smiles and maybe even a few laughs."

Of Media and Messages

If there are two topics that have turned the advertising industry inside out in recent years, they are whether advertising is relevant anymore and if it can be held accountable for results. Those two questions really are the same question, and the answer is the same: "No."

Advertising is no longer relevant and therefore no longer accountable because, in the overwhelming majority of cases, it does not help anyone solve any problems or live a happier life. It is simply an annoyance. Instead of addressing the question of how to make themselves relevant to consumers, advertisers tend to go in the opposite direction, which is to dream up new ways to disrupt our lives with their irrelevant messages.

Advertisers have never encountered an open space that they didn't consider a possible advertising medium. What they fail to understand is that ubiquity and relevance are not the same thing. When everything from egg shells to urinals is being turned into advertising media, something has gone horribly wrong. This desperate attempt to find newfangled media to carry old-fashioned advertising messages is rooted in the decrepit state of the mother of all advertising media: television.

When John Gilbert was vice president of marketing of Dunkin' Donuts (currently he is CMO of TJX Companies), I asked him which media were growing most in importance. He replied with refreshing candor: "This is going to seem like a bit of a strange answer, but TV is growing in importance because it's declining! Our TV effectiveness is declining at about 10 percent a year, but it is still really important as an impact medium. So one of the strategies to deal with that decline is to invest more in it. Obviously, continuing to invest in TV isn't a long-term strategy because at some point even that incremental investment isn't going to get us anything."

John went on to say that he didn't necessarily see the Internet as the answer because "it's difficult to get messages to people who don't want to hear your message. They can ignore you, they can opt out, or they can go to sites where you don't exist."

Some advertisers seem to think the answer is to try to deliver their messages through so many media that you can't possibly ignore them. Others, believing that the problem is the credibility of the media, hope the answer is to use people as media (a.k.a. buzz marketing). Then there are those who think the answer is to have consumers create their own commercials. The thinking apparently is that this will make the ads more relevant. That idea has yet to rise above the level of a gimmick.

Missing from each of these "solutions" is the reality that the problem is not with the medium or with the message. The problem is the outdated idea that using media to carry messages is at the center of the marketing universe. It makes no difference whether your medium is television, radio, magazines, the Internet, the outernet, or somebody's underwear. And it makes no difference whether your message is emotional, funny, or sexy. The very concept of advertising—of media-based message delivery—is no longer as relevant as it used to be.

The really funny part about this is that the true center of the marketing universe is the same as it has always been. As Robert Stephens points out, there is only one thing that's truly relevant to consumers, and it is (drumroll, please) the *product*.

Word of Martin

Chris Martin, the chief executive officer of C. F. Martin & Company, told me that he doesn't do any television advertising for his line of guitars simply because he can't afford it.

He also doesn't really need to advertise because Martin guitars tend to be played by musicians on major television events like the Grammys and the Oscars. "That influences a lot of people," Chris said. "They're like 'Hmm, there must be something to that guitar if Paul Simon is playing one.'" He continued:

"Actually, we do some advertising in the very focused guitar magazines. We run full-page ads that speak to the 'guitar weenie' because it's relevant to them."

But Chris said that the bottom line for him is the response to the warranty card question about the factors that influence a customer's decision to purchase a Martin guitar: "There's a check-the-box for dealer, the ad, and so forth," Chris said. "The box that gets checked more often than not is 'friend.' What a powerful endorsement: 'My friend recommended I buy a Martin guitar.'"

■ **Because Martin guitars are inherently great, it is not necessary to recruit people or pay media vendors to carry the message to others.**

Netflix Clicks

When I spoke with Leslie Kilgore, the chief marketing officer of Netflix, she said she wasn't quite ready to discount the value of advertising in total, but she was quick to add that there was more to success than conveying messages through media.

"While our paid channels, such as television and direct-response vehicles like direct mail, online banners, and search, work extremely hard for us, word of mouth is our best channel," Leslie said. "Eighty-five percent of our new subscribers say that an existing subscriber recommended Netflix to them.

Ninety-three percent of our subscribers say that they evangelize Netflix to friends, family members, and colleagues."

Why? The answer, according to Leslie, was pretty simple: "It all comes back to investing in the customer experience on a 24/7 basis. That's the number-one thing that Netflix invests in."

- **Advertisers should spend less time worrying about the return on investment in their advertising, and more on the return on investment in a relevant customer experience.**

Starbucking Advertising

Starbucks is quite famous for its aversion to traditional advertising. Anne Saunders, before she left Starbucks for Bank of America, told me that the thinking is just very nontraditional:

What we are all about is creating intimate connections with customers, be it in our store or in how we sample our products. Our mass vehicle is sampling; we sample in thirty-five markets, and we'll do it over twelve weeks each year in each of those markets. We'll serve something like 3 million samples this year.

It really is about connecting with someone in a more intimate, experiential way that we think will have longer-lasting ability to build affinity than a thirty-second TV commercial or an ad. Yes, we do some advertising, and we see value in that as well. But I have a team of people who, given our product line, are focused on what we are going to do in the stores and how we communicate that.

You can be extraordinarily successful as a business using what people would call nontraditional means. It has really expanded my view of how one creates awareness and builds loyalty and affinity among customers. It has expanded my notion of how important experience versus information or one-way communications can be.

It is hard to dispute Starbucks' success with its approach. In early 2007, *Advertising Age* reported that Starbucks ranked sixth among the top ten restaurant chains with 1.7 percent market share. McDonald's ranked first with 7.7 percent; however, Starbucks' media expenditure was $16.6 million compared to $727.7 million by McDonald's.

■ **If it's true that the "medium is the message," then the Starbucks message is that media-based advertising communications is not nearly as relevant as it used to be.**

Costco Versus Advertising

Costco's Paul Latham couldn't have been more blunt when I asked him whether Costco had an advertising strategy. "No.

We don't have an advertising budget. None at all. We do some direct mail. Our corporate marketing budget is probably a third of what a company like Microsoft might use to launch a new product."

I followed up by asking him if there were any circumstances under which Costco would do advertising. He responded:

I don't believe so. We haven't done advertising in our thirty years of existence, and that's pretty steadfast. We are asked all the time to pay for placement on various TV shows, but we've found that we get enough exposure on TV, in magazines, and in newspapers without paying for any of it.

Our customers are accustomed to not seeing ads in the newspaper. Sometimes our suppliers or vendors will advertise a product in the newspaper and say that it's available at Costco and other places, but we're very careful to make sure that there's no appearance that Costco is involved in paying for that ad.

Marlboro Country

This may shock you, but if the relationship between media spending and profitable sales volume is the measure, Marlboro cigarettes may be the most accountable brand in marketing history.

As reported in *BusinessWeek* in late 2005, Marlboro owned

"more than 40% of the market, up more than 2.5 percentage points in as many years."

According to Merrill Lynch analyst Christine Farkas, operating profits for Philip Morris (Marlboro's parent) were projected to reach 28 percent in 2006, "from 26 percent in 2004, as net income grew to an estimated $11.4 billion on $66.3 billion in sales in the United States and abroad." At the time that was "twice the current operating margin of well-run companies like General Electric and Exxon-Mobil and also well beyond Procter & Gamble's 19 percent margin."

We don't know exactly how much money Marlboro spent on its marketing to hit those numbers, but Philip Morris acknowledged that it spent less and less on marketing each year. That's because the government won't allow cigarette companies to use mass media to promote their products, which forced Marlboro to innovate and also build a really big database of 26 million of its most loyal customers.

Not only does that approach cost Marlboro a heck of a lot less than mass media advertising, but it also builds a kind of loyalty that television, radio, and print just can't buy. The brand is able to lavish attention on its fan base—up to and including "special trips to a ranch it owns in Montana, where vacationers are showered with gifts, eat five-course meals, drink for free, and enjoy massages, snowmobiling, horseback riding, and the like, all on the company tab."

In other words, Marlboro's customers get to live in Marlboro country versus watching it in thirty-second increments on television—which, when you think about it, is a form of accountability to its consumers in itself.

■ **Marlboro managed to do better and better in terms of the ROI on its marketing expenditures by spending less and less on marketing.**

Motorola's Edge

The late Geoffrey Frost was in the advertising agency business before he moved to the "client side" at Nike and then Motorola, where he was the chief marketing officer. A few months before he passed away, I was lucky enough to spend about an hour on the phone with Geoffrey. At the time, Motorola had just introduced the RAZR, and the brand was flying high.

Geoffrey was all about looking forward. He half-jokingly referred to the cell phone as "the device formerly known as the cell phone" because "it is morphing and evolving so fast into so much more." In light of that, I asked him how his view of advertising had morphed and evolved over the years:

The business obviously has been doing a lot of soul searching. There's an obsession over what is advertising really: Where is it going? I think the big question should be "What isn't advertising?"

Once upon a time, none of the things that advertisers

now take for granted existed. There was no such thing as a radio commercial or a print ad or an outdoor board. They were all created as ways to have a conversation with the public. But in recent years we've heard a lot of talk about "new media" as if there's such a thing as "old" media or that any invention needs a separate category. Just as we are talking about cell phones as "the device formerly known as the cell phone," it might be fun to begin to talk about advertising as "the industry formerly known as advertising."

Sensing controversy, I asked Geoffrey if he thought the advertising industry's obsession with measuring ROI was counterproductive. He replied:

No, I think it's a question of balance. I think it's really important to see what the money you are spending is actually doing. But if you think that there's a magic formula for creating brilliant exceptions, you're crazy.

- **Like the Geek Squad's quality of service, Martin's quality of product, and Starbucks' quality of experience, Motorola's RAZR broke through because of its quality of design. In each case, advertising was all but irrelevant.**

¡Hola! Wachovia

It is worth listening to what Jim Garrity has to say if for no other reason than he held his job as Wachovia's chief marketing officer for more than eighteen months, suggested columnist Jon Fine in *BusinessWeek*. In fact, Jim's tenure—predating Wachovia's merger with First Union—totaled ten years! Jim is now retired from Wachovia, but the reason for his long-term stay in a notoriously short-term job was that he was quite serious about the money he spent on advertising and making sure that each dollar of his "nine-figure marketing budget" was a dollar well spent.

The most obvious result of Jim Garrity's love affair with data points was a notable reduction in spending on broadcast TV. In 2004, Wachovia's broadcast TV budget was $66.8 million, or 37 percent of its total spending, and as of 2006 it was just $53.8 million, or 30 percent of total spending. Jim wouldn't say exactly how he tested for effectiveness but indicated that he liked the Web's "demonstrable" results and confirmed that "Wachovia's pro-golf events and conferences" did quite well.

Jim's challenge was that even though most banks did not make brand evangelists of their customers, it was still pretty "hard to pry people away from established banking relationships." But what Wachovia may have lacked in emotional connectivity, it may have had in customer data and "direct relationships with its roughly 15 million household and business customers."

In any case, Jim Garrity made no secret of which way the

wind was blowing: "If we had wholesale bet the ranch" on what had been learned to date, he told *BusinessWeek*, "we would have allocated 40 percent of the budget significantly differently." Intrigued by that comment, I asked Jim which of the old media he thought had the greatest future potential. I was a little surprised when he said television! His reasoning was that "people really do enjoy the audio-video experience." But he made it clear that he didn't mean "television" in the traditional sense:

The winners will be those with content franchises who figure out how to make their content work seamlessly across platforms. There is no easy way to do that right now. Both the networks and the hardware manufacturers really need to make it seamless. The idea would be to have a central device that stores all your content from the Web, cable, or broadcast and then serves it to multiple high-definition screens and audio-video systems around the house.

- **For Wachovia, success had less to do with creativity and media than it did with forging relevant connections with its customers at each and every touch point.**

Hasta la Vista

The difference between the way Microsoft introduced its Windows 95 operating system twelve years ago and its launch of its new Vista system in early 2007 spoke volumes about changes in marketing communications.

"The assignment in '95 was that we had to convince people the PC mattered and it was going to be part of their life," Microsoft's J. B. Williams said in a *New York Times* article by Louise Story. "Now people are doing this. They're living this digital lifestyle today already." In other words, the launch didn't create the same kind of excitement the second time around.

Yes, there was the obligatory ad campaign, comparing the Vista's arrival to the launch of a spaceship and the demise of the Berlin Wall, suggesting that the only word to describe such events is *wow.* The ad itself didn't quite elicit that kind of response because, as Chuck Porter of Crispin Porter + Bogusky noted, "mass media to a degree doesn't exist anymore."

There also were the obligatory midnight openings, but they didn't attract the same kinds of crowds for Vista that Microsoft garnered for Windows 95. For one thing, there were no shortages as there were for Nintendo's Wii, for example. For another, Vista was available at thirty-nine thousand stores as well as via Amazon.com. Analyst Christopher Swenson of NPD Group commented, "People can get it overnighted to them and delivered to their office. . . . Why would anybody go out in the freezing cold to a retailer?"

The biggest difference between then and now was Microsoft's online strategy, which "focused on three groups of Internet users with different interactive campaigns." For younger consumers there was a MySpace page featuring comedian Demetri

Martin. For techies "Microsoft created a puzzle game called Vanishing Point." And for the general population Microsoft created a site where people could post videos and photos of their favorite "wow" moments.

All told, Microsoft spent some $500,000 on its launch, and while it didn't create much instant excitement, retail analysts said they expected Vista to sell just fine over the long run.

■ **When a megabrand like Microsoft spends just a half million dollars on a major new product launch, it is time to think twice about where and how we are investing our marketing dollars.**

indiOne Hotels

"We haven't spent a rupee on advertising," said R. K. Krishna Kumar, vice chairman of Indian Hotels, as quoted by Pete Engardio in *BusinessWeek*.

He hadn't had to because at his indiOne Hotel chain in Bangalore, the rooms come with free wireless and flat-panel TVs but cost only $22 a night. Elsewhere in Bangalore you would be lucky to get a room in a second-rate hotel for less than $200. This was not just another story about the power of word-of-mouth marketing versus advertising, however. The larger story was the lengths to which Indian Hotels had gone to deliver such an astonishing value.

Led by C. K. Prahalad, a management guru, indiOne took aim at reinventing the budget hotel by drastically reducing the costs involved in running it. Where a typical U.S. motel has a staff of about 50 and a luxury hotel employs about 130, the indiOne was getting by with just 7 employees. Most of the hotel services were outsourced, and most reservations were made online.

Even at its extraordinarily low room rate, indiOne posted "operating margins of 65 percent, compared with about 35 percent for four-star Taj Hotels and 50 percent for five-star properties."

■ **Abandoning advertising isn't just a tactic for indiOne Hotels; it is part of the brand's business model.**

Brooklyn Industries

Lexy Funk and Vahap Avsar grew their eight-store fashion boutique, Brooklyn Industries, by cutting their advertising budget in half. Actually, their overall marketing budget continued to represent about 2 percent of their revenues, as it always had. It is just that instead of spending their dollars on ads, Lexy and Vahap invested in better window displays and fancier catalogs.

"We were shocked to see how little impact our ads had," Vahap told Beth Kwon of *Inc.* magazine. Research revealed that most of their customers "were first drawn to Brooklyn Industries by spotting one of its eight stores in Brooklyn and Manhattan." So the new plan was to refresh their displays twelve times a year instead of just ten.

Lexy and Vahap also poured more resources into their catalogs. In 2006 they put out four catalogs, forty-eight pages each, and printed twenty-two thousand. In 2007 they produced five catalogs, sixty-four pages each, and printed thirty thousand. They also thought about "printing on better paper and in a larger format."

Lexy and Vahap said they didn't "expect the catalogs to produce a lot of sales." Their main hope was that the catalogs would find a place on customer coffee tables and, like their window displays, have greater impact than ads. Lexy said, "When you advertise through store windows and catalogs, you can speak directly to the customer."

- **The more directly Brooklyn Industries connected to its customers' daily lives (that is, from their neighborhoods to their coffee tables), the more effective its marketing became.**

Patagonia's Pages

Patagonia, the outdoor lifestyle brand, also invests heavily in catalogs and shares Lexy and Vahap's belief that the primary goal is not necessarily to sell products per se. As Rick Ridgeway, Patagonia's president of communications, once explained to me, the real goal is not to advertise your stuff but to connect with your customers. He said:

> I would doubt that there are many other companies that devote between 40 and 50 percent of their catalog to non-selling space. As much as half of our catalog real estate goes into essays and stories about customers using our products, the adventures they've had, and our own commitment to providing solutions to the environmental crisis.
>
> Our ad budget is about 4 percent at this point. That's pretty low for most companies. The most valuable marketing of all, as everyone knows, is word of mouth. In fact, we know that 52 percent of our new customers come to us through word of mouth.
>
> You can achieve that kind of word of mouth best when you are an authentic brand, an authentic company. The return that Patagonia enjoys comes from the people who become so loyal that they almost proselytize our brand for us.

■ **Authenticity is the new advertising.**

Shopper Science

When Dr. Joshua Freedman conducted brain scans of people watching television commercials, he found that "a third to a half of commercials do not generate any brain reaction at all," reported Kenneth Chang in the *New York Times*.

Dr. Freedman also found that those commercials that did get the synapses firing created conflict. "Almost always if you activated one part of the brain . . . you activated many competing parts of the brain," he said. In other words, your commercial might "activate not only the orbitofrontal cortex and the ventral stratium [translation: the part of the brain that creates desire] but also the amygdala, the part of the brain associated with fear and anxiety"—which would stop cold any thoughts of running out and buying your product.

■ **The most surprising thing about this report is that only a third of television commercials failed to create a brain reaction.**

Nike Life

"We are not in the business of keeping the media companies alive," said Nike's Trevor Edwards in a *New York Times* article by Louise Story. "We're in the business of connecting with consumers."

Count Linda Martello among the consumers grateful to Nike for that kind of connection. She said the connection actually helped her nurse an injured calf muscle. Of course, Nike's advice was to switch to a pair of Nike-brand shoes. But that hardly mattered to Linda because it solved her problem and enabled her to participate in Nike's thrice-weekly runs in Central Park.

The events actually were just one part of Nike's strategy to build its brand by ingratiating itself—rather than advertising—to its consumers. "We want to find a way to enhance the experience and services, rather than looking for a way to interrupt people from getting to where they want to go," said Nike's Stephan Olander.

Unlike the olden days when news, entertainment, or other "content" were the services, for Nike the service increasingly was about helping people get the most out of Nike's products. That meant more of Nike's marketing dollars were being invested in "physical interaction" with its brands and less in traditional advertising.

Nike did increase "its spending on traditional media in the United States by 3 percent from 2003 to 2006," but its investment in nonmedia activities increased by 33 percent. What that meant was Nike spent way more on nonmedia marketing ($457.9 million) than traditional media ($220.5 million). As of 2007, Nike's spending on traditional media was down 55 percent compared to ten years earlier. While live events such as the Central Park run were a big part of Nike's shift, the brand also invested in online initiatives designed to bring its customers together both online and off.

Perhaps best of all when that happens—when Nike's swoosh-festooned athletes get together for a run—they become, for all intents and purposes, "a human billboard" for the brand.

■ **By focusing on solving its customers' problems and
    bringing them together for special events, Nike
    literally made its customers both the medium and the
    message.**

Hollywood Buzz

What propels theatrical box office? Well, you might be surprised to hear that the answer is not buzz marketing, it's
awareness, wrote Adam Leipzeig in the *New York Times*. In
fact, "in most cases, nearly half of a movie's total audience
turns out in the first week of release, which means there has
been very little or no word of mouth motivating most of the
audience." Increasingly, the initial awareness is driven less by
ad campaigns than by movies with familiar names (that is,
sequels).

Whatever buzz there is doesn't happen until opening night,
but when it does, it does so with sickening speed as "teenagers . . .
send a text message to friends during the first show on Friday
about whether a film is good or bad."

■ **Most of the potential audience for any given film has
    decided whether or not to see it within twenty-four hours
    of its release, so any advertising after that point is largely
    irrelevant.**

Trial and Repeat

The effects of rapid-fire word of mouth on traditional as-
sumptions about how marketing works have given pause
to Donna Sturgess, global head of innovation at GlaxoSmith-
Kline. Specifically, Donna said she's been thinking about how
word of mouth affects the traditional notions of "trial and
repeat":

> In a television model we would send messages to get con-
> sumers to go to the store to try our products and then buy it
> again, hopefully. However, in a word-of-mouth world we
> almost have to put the "repeat" before the "trial" because
> the chances are now greater that consumers won't even try
> a product unless they've heard about it from someone else
> via word of mouth first.
>
> In other words, a consumer's decision to try a product
> may be based on someone else's verdict as to whether a
> product is worth buying a second time. So, in effect, the
> product has to stand up to performance on repeat pur-
> chases in order to generate more trial.
>
> A marketer could spend a lot of money to get a trial
> through television advertising but fail to get the trial be-
> cause the repeat cycle—based on word of mouth—is now
> kicking in much faster. That also means there is no more
> room for products that are all sizzle and no steak because
> they will be discredited faster.

■ **Marketing's new mantra may be repeat and trial, not trial and repeat.**

Assault on Advertising

Al Gore may be a visionary on global warming. He may have brilliantly parlayed his epic electoral loss into $100 million in personal net worth. Who knows, he may even be "reelected" president someday. But in his 2007 book, *The Assault on Reason*, Al Gore missed the boat on the present state of television advertising in general and its true status relative to America's democratic process in particular.

Nobody questions the dominant role of thirty-second television commercials in political campaigns. About $2 billion was expected to be spent on television ads during the 2008 election cycle. As Mr. Gore himself noted, something like 80 to 90 percent of the money raised by candidates is used to buy TV time. What he failed to recognize was what a colossal waste of money that is. Instead, he stretched back to his 1984 Senate campaign for anecdotal evidence of the "power" of television advertising: "[M]y campaign advisers made a recommendation and prediction that surprised me with its specificity: 'If you run this ad at this many "points" [a measure of the advertising buy], and if [your opponent] responds as we anticipate and then we purchase this many points to air our response to his response, the net result after three weeks will be an increase of 8.5 percent in your lead in the polls.'"

So that's what the Gore campaign did—and guess what? After three weeks his lead increased by exactly 8.5 percent, just as his advisers said it would.

With all due respect, 1984 was a really long time ago. Back in those days, Mount Kilimanjaro still had snow. Long gone is the time when you could predict that kind of result with that kind of precision. In fact, the only thing for certain about traditional television advertising these days is that it does not provide a reliable return on marketing investment. Indeed, a survey by *The Hub* magazine found that about 70 percent of senior-level marketers agree the effectiveness of traditional TV advertising is not what it used to be.

Obviously, the Internet is a key driver of the media fragmentation that has rendered television advertising less effective than it used to be. At the same time its powerful potential to connect with consumers is a driving force behind its own extraordinary growth as a marketing medium.

One would think that the former vice president, with his early and intense interest in the "information superhighway," would understand this better than most people. However, a quick read of his book's acknowledgments reveals that while he consulted with numerous experts in constitutional law, neuroscience, psychology, history, the Internet, and the environment, he apparently didn't take the time to talk to anyone in the advertising business. The result is an otherwise thoughtful and persuasive book about the decline of reason in political discourse that misses the mark where the role of television advertising in American life is concerned.

The issue Mr. Gore raised isn't limited to whether television commercials produce measurable results, either. There is a larger matter here that goes to the very heart of the future of marketing itself. Al Gore's premise is that because television advertising is so powerful, it is evil. While he admitted he was happy that his television ads worked, he also said he was troubled by how easily voters were manipulated. His point was that television advertising—and, by extension, marketing itself—was all about tricking people.

In this case he went back not just twenty-three years but more than fifty years—to the writings of John Kenneth Galbraith—to make his point: "In the 1950s, John Kenneth Galbraith first described the way in which advertising altered the classical relationship by which supply and demand are balanced over time by the invisible hand of the marketplace. Modern advertising campaigns, he pointed out, were beginning to create high levels of demand for products that consumers never knew they wanted, much less needed."

That may have been very true at the time (and sometimes is still true today). Yes, the business of marketing may well be about promoting things we never knew we wanted or needed (did anyone ever ask for an iPod?) but only within the context of what is relevant to the way we live our lives today. Any other approach is doomed to failure.

Al Gore is probably right that the level of political dialogue in this country is at an all-time low. It may be true that what citizens really want and need from our government (both parties and all branches) is being ignored as never before. I couldn't agree more that the more engaged citizenry that Al Gore advocates is essential to a successful democracy. But the problem is not the power of advertising, it is the weakness of politicians who use "social networks" to raise billions of dollars on the Internet, only to short-circuit that conversation and waste their money on outdated, ineffective, negative, and often outright insulting television advertising campaigns.

■ **Relevance in marketing is not about manipulating us as much as it is about serving us. And that's the inconvenient truth.**

The Ultimate Accountability

Few in the advertising business talk much about Marshall McLuhan anymore, probably because nobody ever really understood what he was talking about in the first place. Even he didn't claim to get it all. "My stuff is very difficult," he once said.

McLuhan is most famous, of course, for the notion that how we receive information is more important than the information itself—or, as he put it, "Societies have always been shaped more by the nature of the media by which men communicate

than by the content of the communication." People mostly remember this concept as "the medium is the message."

The idea of the "medium as message" (or "massage" if you
prefer the typo, as McLuhan did) is more relevant today than
ever. It is just that the context of the concept is not what it was
forty years ago. McLuhan was talking about the relatively new
medium of television, as compared to the old media of radio
and print, and how the differences changed how messages were
received.

The medium is indeed still the message, but today the media are the products or services themselves and not any media-
based advertising overlay.

If you are looking through that prism, the whole debate
over advertising and accountability really has missed the point.
The point is that true accountability in marketing really has
nothing to do with marketing-mix models or proving to the
CEO, the CFO, and board of directors that the dollars spent on
this medium or that medium paid off in dollars and cents.

■ **The ultimate accountability in marketing is not how
efficiently or effectively advertising dollars are spent; it is
how relevant the brand is to the consumer.**

PART II

·

Relevant Solutions

CHAPTER 4

Insights

Controlling the Conversation

Propaganda ends where dialogue begins.
—Marshall McLuhan

My first job after graduating from college was as a disc jockey at a 50,000-watt FM radio station called WDJF in Westport, Connecticut. Naturally, I started out working nights, the graveyard shift. My pretty blond girlfriend married me anyway.

Being on the air was a strange and wonderful experience. I was alone in a room—for all intents and purposes talking to myself—and yet I was heard by thousands of people at a time. During a break I'd pick up the phone. On the line was a listener, a total stranger, who would speak to me as if I were the closest of friends. And why not? That's the way I had been speaking to the listener. Radio's power is in that kind of one-to-one communication. The commercials sandwiched between the music and my patter did not capitalize on that connection, however. More often than not the ads actually disrupted things. If anything, the ads were so jarring and abrasive that they undermined whatever credibility I might have had.

Radio is a fantastic medium. In fact, it is my favorite medium, which is why it makes me so sad to see it wasted as just another way to clutter our lives with so much irrelevant advertising. Actually, I've often thought that radio's abuse as a cheap vessel for ads instead of a priceless channel for meaningful conversation is emblematic of much of what's wrong with marketing today.

If that last statement didn't give you pause, please read it again.

Radio, Radio

You may have heard of KEXP, an experimental radio station that has been exploring radio's true potential for some thirty-five years.

According to an article by Brier Dudley in the *Seattle Times,* Microsoft cofounder Paul Allen provides funding for the station via his Experience Music Project, a museum of music he built in Seattle. Originally, KEXP was a radio station doubling as a technology laboratory, but it may turn out to be a model for the future of radio itself.

Over the years KEXP has introduced a range of innovations, such as the ability to broadcast CD-quality music and to archive broadcasts online so that listeners can tune to their favorite programs at their convenience. In 2007, KEXP's Tom Mara said the station was contemplating "some type of social network for its listeners so they can discuss new music and perhaps share photos and videos." Something similar is already happening online at music-oriented social-network sites like Mog.com and Last.fm, which enable members to not only meet other people with similar musical tastes but also view music videos based on the songs in their music libraries.

In another interesting experiment, UltraRadio.com operates an online-only classic-rock radio station out of a storefront in New Haven, Connecticut. Backed by sixteen investors, a former radio ad-sales guy named Randy Borovsky based his station on building a community.

UltraRadio does accept ads, albeit just six minutes of spots per hour versus twelve to fifteen on broadcast radio. Even more important, as reported in the *New York Times*, the station became "a centerpiece of the local rock scene, playing music from any one of more than 150 Connecticut bands at least once an hour and nothing but local music for eight hours overnight."

That's not unlike what radio great Murray the K did back in the 1950s and 1960s. Peter Altschuler, one of Murray's sons, told me that when his famous father wasn't on the air, "he was in clubs listening to what his audience was listening to—before they were listening to it on the air, before the groups had recording contracts, before their first record was cut. It was field research of the most basic kind."

When radio is approached with that kind of intensity, with such extraordinary personal dedication to the interests of its audience, its ability to sell to that audience is hard to match.

■ **Marketers in search of relevance should take a look at radio as a possible model for how conversations could build their brands.**

Idol Conversations

Ever think about why *American Idol* became so popular? I have, and I suspect that it is because the program's very premise was that the viewers controlled the story line—more or less, that is. In reality, *American Idol* won by merely creating the *illusion* of consumer empowerment.

American Idol's first dirty little secret was that only a small percentage of the people who watched the show actually voted for their favorite singers. A viewer survey by Initiative, a media and marketing communications network, found, surprisingly, that the opportunity to vote was actually the least engaging aspect of the show.

The second not-so-secret secret was that the show's judges—Simon Cowell especially—were there to subvert what America actually wanted and make sure the "correct" contestant won. The problem was that it didn't always work out exactly as planned. In the show's fifth season, an "incorrect" contestant, Constantine Maroulis, attempted to bypass *American Idol*'s idea of a story line by creating his own.

How did he do that? It was pretty simple, actually. Constantine was reading what his fans were saying on the *American Idol* blog and taking their lead. If his fans asked him to wear his hair in a ponytail, that's what he did. If they sent him five dozen roses and asked him to wear one on the show, he did that, too. I asked Constantine about his strategy:

> *I tried to pick up on what the fans were interested in and how they were viewing me. My brother and I would liaise every day. He'd be surfing the 'Net and getting the vibe of what was out there. I'd try to feed my fans just enough of what they wanted to keep them really, really interested. For example, fans were teasing me about how I was this modern-day David Cassidy type. For the moms it was like a blast into the past of the '70s. They just remembered what it was like when they were kids, and I gave them sort of that feeling. So I took the piss out of them and did a Partridge Family song on the show.*

The show's judges didn't seem to appreciate it, though, and ultimately Constantine's interactive storytelling couldn't compete with *American Idol*'s presumptive plot line. In fact, he was eliminated from the competition earlier than most people expected. But that's beside the point.

■ **Constantine's branding was all about having a conversation with his consumers, and he set a good example for others to follow.**

Blog *This*

It is doubtful that many brands would take Constantine's cue because, frankly, so many marketers seem to be afraid of what their consumers have to say. Just look at corporate America's initial reaction to blogging: Rather than encouraging a true dialogue, much of branded America was instead intent on controlling the conversation. Indeed, an article in *Business-Week* suggested that a good chunk of the marketing world's energy is negative when it comes to blogs. In the main they are "monitoring" blogs for bad news and "buttonholing" bloggers for the purposes of "damage control."

But what exactly is the nature of the damage? That consumers are telling their versions of a brand's story? That Constantine should win instead of Carrie or Bo? That's not damage; it's insight.

Good marketers have always had conversations with their consumers through focus groups, surveys, and other research techniques. But like a lot of what happens in marketing, the dialogue tends to be a tactic, not a strategy. The conversation starts and stops at the pleasure of the marketer, who firmly controls the context every step of the way. Doesn't that make it harder to be innovative? It would sure seem so.

As Yahoo!'s Jeff Weiner told *BusinessWeek*: "I'm amazed people don't get it yet. . . . Never in the history of market research has there been a tool like [blogs]."

It's like Ruth Ann Manners (my mother) once told me, "Creativity is about changing someone else's idea into your own." Isn't that what we marketers try to do each and every day? Why not invite our customers to join in on the fun?

■ **Relevant brands let their best customers in on the creativity by inviting a conversation.**

Dell's Bells

Conversing with your consumers may be just lip service for some companies, but for Dell it was central to a rejuvenated reputation, wrote Jeff Jarvis in *BusinessWeek*. In 2006, Dell's internal tracking reported customer satisfaction among core users at just 58 percent. Satisfaction among high-end customers was even worse. Michael Dell went "ballistic," said Dick Hunter, head of Dell's customer service.

A year later Dell's core customer satisfaction was up to 74 percent, and the high end had jumped to 80 percent. That still wasn't good enough, but those numbers apparently would not have been as high if it weren't for Dell's blog, Direct2Dell.com. "I think what the Web has brought is the voice of that 25 percent," said Dick.

Dell launched Direct2Dell.com in July 2006, "where chief blogger Lionel Menchaca gave the company a frank and credible human voice." That happened only after the company had been thoroughly flamed by unhappy customers online. At that point Michael Dell was encouraged by Jeff Jarvis to "join the conversation your customers are having without you." Dell started by dispatching "technicians to reach out to complaining bloggers and solve their problems, earning pleasantly surprised buzz in return." Direct2Dell was launched amid "a burning battery issue," and shortly afterward Michael Dell himself started IdeaStorm.com, a blog asking "customers to tell the company what to do."

In response to their advice, Dell began "selling Linux computers and reducing the promotional 'bloatware' that clogs machines," which allowed its "customers to rate its products on its site." It also streamlined its call center support.

Mark Jarvis, Dell's new CMO, said he regarded Dell's customer conversations as its strategy. "By listening to our customers, that is actually the most perfect form of marketing you could have." His boss regarded it as an engine of innovation.

"I'm sure there's a lot of things that I can't even imagine but our customers can imagine," said Michael Dell, adding, "A company this size is not going to be about a couple of people coming up with ideas. It's going to be about millions of people and harnessing the power of those ideas."

■ **For Dell, listening instead of talking revived its image, boosted its innovation, and restored its relevance.**

Customer Creativity

Conversations can lead directly to innovations. Indeed, about three-quarters of attempts at innovation fail because of the way corporations go about it, said Eric Von Hippel of the Massachusetts Institute of Technology, as reported by *The Economist*. According to Eric, author of a book called *Democratizing Innovation*, the mistake is that firms typically send market researchers into the field to identify "unmet needs" and then turn the results over to product development teams. He said they should instead identify "the few special customers who innovate" and invite them to brainstorm the possibilities.

That is the way GE's healthcare does it. GE calls these special customers "luminaries," and they meet regularly to discuss GE's latest technologies and how to turn them into products.

Staples, the office supplies retailer, has applied a similar concept but in a different way. It held "a competition among customers to come up with new ideas. It received eighty-three hundred submissions," according to Michael Collins of Big Idea Group, which helped Staples stage the competition. One result was a product called "wordlock—a padlock that uses words instead of numbers." A few years ago BMW "posted a toolkit on its Web site" that allowed its customers to suggest ways in which the carmaker "could take advantage of advances in telematic and in-car online services." About fifteen of the one thousand customers who used the kit were invited to meet with BMW's engineers in Munich, and some of the resulting ideas moved on to the concept stage.

Sometimes, however, the customer innovation happens whether the marketer asked for it or not. For example, back in 1997, LEGO was about three weeks away from launching a "build-it-yourself robot development system" called Mindstorms when about one thousand hackers "downloaded its operating system, vastly improved it, and posted their work freely online. After a long stunned silence, LEGO accepted the merits of this community's work: Programs written in hacker language were uploaded to the Mindstorms Web site." It seems one person's hacker can be another's open-source software developer.

In any case, as Eric Von Hippel noted, the concept doesn't cost much because many customers consider being "listened to" compensation enough. As BMW's Jörg Reimann explained, "They were so happy to be invited by us and that our technical experts were interested in their ideas. They didn't want any money."

■ **Your best customers can also be your best innovators.**

Let's Talk

What is the best way to have a conversation with your customers? I asked a few master communicators from Audi, Colgate-Palmolive, and WomanWise.

Stephen Berkov, formerly of Audi
(currently of Edmunds.com)

One thing that I find particularly helpful is the experiential marketing event. We have events where we invite prospects, owners, and the media. Our focus is on the *quality* of the experience and getting exactly the right people to attend.

We create an experience where current Audi owners feel at home, and the friends they're bringing to consider Audi are also relaxed. The environment is warm and open. People are comfortable because we're hitting their passion points, and they open up. We get great feedback on what they like or don't like about our product and campaigns.

Jim Figura, Colgate-Palmolive

I believe that there's no single best way, but I also believe the entire marketing and sales organization must be engaged in the process. At Colgate everyone in the organization has a specific objective that is tied to their bonuses around what's called "getting external."

The objective can cover consumer immersion, shopper marketing, and other activities that put our people in direct contact with consumers, shoppers, our suppliers, even raw material suppliers, and, even more important, the retailer.

Dori Molitor, WomanWise

We have developed several techniques that are designed to get at the subconscious motivators of consumer behavior. For example, we use what we call "girlfriend groups," which are designed to tap into the way women naturally give and ask for advice.

It is an informal, casual environment where we have a group of women who are girlfriends get together. We moderate a discussion and also introduce a variety of projective exercises, such as role playing. The overall point is to get at that single subconscious emotional truth that drives the consumer's relationship with your brand.

Bang & Innovation

The greatest strength of electronics maker Bang & Olufsen is that its designers don't consider either consumers or engineers, as Jay Greene reported in *BusinessWeek*. It is also the company's greatest weakness.

B&O's approach enabled it to earn wide margins from "well-heeled consumers who want to buy originality and quality from an exclusive brand. That's how the company [fifty-six stores in the United States, fourteen hundred worldwide] generated $96.6 million in operating profits before taxes in the fiscal year ended May 31, [2007], up 22 percent from the year before."

However, "B&O's business-by-genius MO is a fragile model" that "depends on the instincts of a handful of quirky and creative individuals and the ability of executives to manage them."

B&O's designers don't "do even the basic market research ethnography common among consumer-oriented companies" because they believe that "consumers often don't really know what they want." The trouble is that sometimes B&O's designers don't know, either. For example, B&O's BeoSound 2 was meant to compete against the iPod. Priced at $460, it holds just fifty songs and has no screen. David Lewis, its designer, figured that with so few songs on the drive, "consumers wouldn't need a screen to navigate their music." Uh-oh. The BeoSound 2 tanked.

The problem was that David designed the device without knowing enough about the technology—specifically, that memory capacity was exploding. That could be because B&O designers think the only use for engineers is to figure out how to execute what the designers design.

■ **Bang & Olufsen's successes and failures suggest that there can be a fine line between arrogance and relevance.**

Lafley's Curve

That's Alan George Lafley, as in A. G. Lafley, as in the CEO of consumer products giant Procter & Gamble. Alan George— that's how the man introduces himself to consumers as he follows them into their homes to find out what kind of shampoo they have in their bathtubs, as reported by Luisa Kroll in *Forbes*. Yes, he really does this. He thinks one of P&G's biggest issues is that it is too far removed from its consumers and that the best way to fix that is by talking directly to them himself.

Lafley arrived at this conclusion while running P&G's operations in the Far East where there was no consumer data in which to bury his head. His best bet was to visit stores and homes, and he "learned, for example, that shoppers hated Max Factor for being garish and foreign." He also commented, "I don't think the answers are just in numbers. You have to get out and look." He has even colored hair (not his own), coming away impressed by how complicated it is. "Women have to give up half a day and have their best friend along," he observed. "I'm sure we can improve on this."

Said Lafley, "I am a broken record when it comes to saying, 'We have to focus on the consumer.'" He added, "It's really a very simple business."

■ **Procter & Gamble's A. G. Lafley not only listens to what his customers say but he also watches what they do.**

Mon Quotidien

Mon Quotidien, a newspaper in France, took an interesting and very brave approach to the consumer conversation. According to an article in the *Christian Science Monitor*, the paper invited kids to participate in its twice weekly editorial meetings and actually gave them veto power over what was published. Sometimes the results were wildly counterintuitive. For example, on a day when the story choices included an "important" election and an "unimportant" bear in a zoo, the kids chose to lead with the bear story. The paper always went with what the kids selected, and as a result *Mon Quotidien* found itself growing at a time when many other papers were not.

■ **Trusting kids to call the shots took courage, but the payoff for *Mon Quotidien* was big.**

Rocking the Jolly Roger

The issue of piracy is the ultimate conversation stopper. It kind of puts a damper on things when a marketer says, "You're under arrest." All that does is give the consumer the right to remain silent, which doesn't exactly encourage a dialogue. But that's what marketers in the music business have done.

It has mostly been the creative types in the equation—the artists who are, in effect, the brands—who understand the relevance of piracy as part of the conversation they are having with their fans.

Let's start with Prince. In 2004, Prince played to piracy impulses by giving away a copy of his latest CD, *Musicology*, with every ticket sold to one of his concerts. The kicker was that he convinced SoundScan, which tracks record sales, to count the giveaways as "sold" CDs. That sent *Musicology* charging up the charts, which gave Prince more radio airplay, more publicity, and more displays at retail. The result, of course, was more sales. Well, that was just a little too much success for Sound-Scan, which quickly announced it would not allow anybody else to do what Prince had done. This seems to be a pattern in the record business: If it outwits the rules, outlaw it.

What Prince did was possible because of a highly innovative record deal under which he was paid no advance but retained artistic control as well as ownership of his master recordings. The deal not only gave Prince the freedom to record whatever he wanted and give away CDs, but also to distribute his work via his Web site, where fans could download *Musicology* for a low-cost, onetime fee.

"I don't really take a stance on piracy," Prince told *USA Today*. "If I was only getting a few pennies off every album, I'd be worried. But I get $7 a pop for every album that sells for $10. That's enough."

That would be more than enough for Wilco, the pop combo, which, incredibly, chose to pirate its own work. Having been fired by its record label over artistic differences (yet another pattern here), the band streamed its 2001 collection, *Yankee Hotel Foxtrot*, online for free. By the time the record was released for sale by Wilco's new label, Nonesuch Records, it was so well known and loved that it promptly hit No. 8 on the *Billboard* charts, which was better than any of the group's previous records had done.

"Treating your audience like thieves is absurd," Wilco's Jeff Tweedy told *Wired* magazine. In fact, in a remarkable display of the true colors of truly loyal consumers, some of Wilco's fans were so grateful for the free tunes that they actually asked to send some money for it—which the band accepted and forwarded (a total of about $15,000) to Doctors Without Borders, a charity.

In the same interview, Jeff made the key point that the resolution of online music is not as high quality as the offline kind. It is a point that ex-Byrd Roger McGuinn had made about four years earlier in testimony before the U.S. Senate at the height of the Napster controversy. Hailing the Internet as "the radio of the twenty-first century," Roger implied that those who saw piracy as a threat simply hadn't considered its place as part of the consumer conversation. As Roger later told me: "I don't think they get it. You know, when you get your songs played on the radio, people can tape that, and the quality is just about as good as an MP3. . . . I've only gained exposure through the Internet, as opposed to losing record sales."

That exposure has mostly been of Roger's own making. Way back in 1995 he launched FolkDen.com, where each and every month since he has posted a song that his fans can download for free. In 2005 he capitalized on his hard-earned online presence by forming his own record label, April First Productions, and releasing a new rock album, *Limited Edition*—so named because it is available for sale online only. In a few short months *Limited Edition*, via limited online distribution, made more money than Roger's previous major-label hit record, *Back from Rio*, which, despite having sold more than half a million copies, never returned a dime in royalties to him.

Although Roger said he didn't have the data to determine a direct correlation between free FolkDen.com downloads and *Limited Edition* sales, he said he had picked some of the songs for the record based on their popularity as downloads. Encouraged by robust sales as well as glowing reviews, Roger later marketed a CD-quality boxed set of the more than one hundred songs otherwise available for free on FolkDen.com.

Sales and marketing innovation based on an enlightened view of piracy is not the exclusive domain of the artists, of course. Wilco's financial success was based on a subsequent record deal with Nonesuch, and Prince's strategic subversion was premised on distribution via Columbia Records.

Remember what advertising legend David Ogilvy said? He said a lot of very smart things, but this is one of my favorites: "The consumer is not an idiot. She is your wife." Were David Ogilvy alive to witness the present-day collision of piracy and consumerism, he might have added, "The consumer is not a criminal. She is your consumer."

■ **Where some marketers see "piracy," artists like Prince, Jeff Tweedy, and Roger McGuinn hear a "conversation."**

Disney's Dialogue

Just how complex it can be to have a truly relevant conversation with your customer came home to me when I spoke with Tom Boyles, the senior vice president of global customer-managed relationships for Disney Theme Parks and Resorts. The first thing to note about Tom is his job title: "customer-*managed* relationships." At most companies, his title would be "customer relationship *management*."

The difference is more than just semantics, said Tom. "The change to 'customer-*managed* relationships' brings into greater focus the idea that our guests are taking a greater and greater amount of control in the relationships they choose to establish with us." In other words, Disney's idea was that it is the customer who manages their relationships with Disney, not the other way around. For Disney it was a critical difference because the degree to which the customer was in control was the difference between having a great vacation or not.

To accomplish that, Disney engaged its customers in an extended and very detailed conversation. As Tom explained:

If you contact us via the Web or through the call center, twenty-four hours later we have sent out an email to you that basically reinforces what you said you were interested in doing, and presents some additional information and recommendations on how to make your trip as good as it can be.

If you call us back and book, within twenty-four hours we send you a customized, four-page letter that reiterates the information that you shared with us. We'll also make recommendations based on what you told us.

We don't just give you the latest thing we're trying to push. It's all very much based on what you told us, the ages of your kids, whether or not you've been here before, right down to your favorite characters and attractions.

The conversation continued after the guest arrived at Disney:

We'll be able to help you get the most out of your visit in real time, whether through . . . a cell phone or a PDA. For example, if you said you're interested in a certain attraction, and we know that the attraction is running slower than normal, there's an opportunity for us to alert you about that.

The same is true of dining reservations and bus schedules—all of that is in the vision of where we will take the next step of this CMR solution. . . . The idea that the technology is now enabling you to have the ability to man-

age the relationship even better than before is critically important.

The bottom line, said Tom, was this:

If we can make the experience really cool and interesting, and if you're not walking around the park stressed out because you're not sure what to do next—if we can make that experience better for you—not only do you get a better trip, but we get a more likely outcome that you'll return.

The right way to the right business solution for us is through providing rich guest experiences that keep getting better, that exceed expectations. . . . That's the same philosophy that permits me to put guests at the center of what we do and try to communicate with them in a relevant and meaningful way.

■ **For Disney, knowing what to do next to make every vacation a perfect vacation depends on putting its guests in control of the conversation.**

Ketchup F——up

Everybody talks about "user-generated content," but it seems that Heinz may be wishing it had never invited its consumers into that conversation, as reported by Louise Story in the *New*

York Times. It must have seemed like a good idea to ask consumers to create their own Heinz Ketchup commercial. After all, Doritos, Converse, Dodge, and others had done it. The prize was $57,000. The promise was that five of the best entries would be shown on television.

What Heinz didn't count on was that very few if any consumers who entered the contest seemed to think about Heinz's advertising the way Heinz did. Maybe Heinz wasn't ready for consumers like twenty-year-old Dan Burke, for example. "I just thought to myself, 'What is the single strangest thing I can do with ketchup?'" said Dan. His answer was to brush his teeth and shave his face with it. Another hopeful "rubs ketchup over his face like acne cream and then puts pickles on his eyes," while yet another "ends with a close-up of a mouth with crooked yellow teeth."

In many of the videos the ketchup looked more like blood than anything else. Not all the submissions were gross; many were rejected for other reasons, such as running longer than thirty seconds. On top of it all, Heinz was accused by some of being cheap and lazy for asking its consumers to come up with their advertising. According to Heinz vice president David Ciesinski, however, the user-generated ads actually were "at least as expensive if not more" than agency-generated ads, in part because Heinz promoted its contest on *American Idol* and "converted all the labels on its bottles and ketchup packets into ads for the contest" at big expense. The contest also involved a lot of work for Heinz because it had to slog through all those entries.

Ultimately, the real issue was that so many of the ads had nothing to do with how consumers felt about ketchup. In interviews, some contestants said that they preferred mustard or mayonnaise. And it may have had everything to do with how they felt about cash prizes. "It is a substantial sum of money, which, of course, caught my eye," said Michelle Cale. As for Dan Burke, he said he hoped to spend his winnings on wrestling lessons.

■ **Letting your consumers create your ads might not make advertising any more relevant.**

In Another League

In fairness, other advertisers, such as the National Football League, also invited consumers to create their own ads and achieved a happier result. I asked Lisa Baird, when she was the NFL's senior vice president of marketing and consumer products, whether consumer-generated ads wasn't just a fad:

> *I definitely have heard that critique, but when you are face-to-face and are hearing a fan's story about what we should tell our fans on the Super Bowl, the last thing on your mind is that we're sitting there doing this because it's a fad.*
>
> *NFL fans have fantastic ideas, they love our sport, and*

they're passionate about their teams. The NFL is like oxy-
gen to people. . . . When you sit there and listen to that fan,
you think, "You know what? Something special could come
out of this."

At the end of the day that is what we want—a really
special story about a really special fan. I don't think that's a
fad at all. We posted outtakes of some of the ads our fans
have created, and they just put a smile on your face.

How Much Is Too Much?

How much control should consumers have in shaping brand
identity? I asked folks from JetBlue Airways, Allstate Insur-
ance, Visa U.S.A., and Euro RSCG Chicago.

Andrea Spiegel, JetBlue

The JetBlue brand identity was built so quickly because of
word of mouth, which shaped who we are today. We welcome
an open dialogue with our customers. If we're hearing a universal belief or suggestion, we will take it very seriously and
make changes based on it. However, there is a bit of a danger in
giving consumers too much control because at the end of the
day you have to run your business the way it needs to be run,
based on your expertise.

Giving customers control doesn't mean that they should
necessarily create your advertising. In fact, I think that the

more we see that happening, the less of an appetite there's going to be for it.

Joe Tripodi, formerly of Allstate (currently of Coca-Cola Co.)
Fundamentally, the consumer should have some control in shaping the brand identity, but clearly the consumer is not going to be creating a communication strategy. Utlimately, the consumer is going to be rooted in the foundation of what the brand stands for, and that's what the marketer needs to communicate. Where some brands get into trouble is when there's a huge gap between the stimuli—the marketing communication—and the actual customer experience.

Kellie Krug, formerly of Visa
(currently of Common Sense Media)
Visa recently embarked on a mobile-phone pilot with AT&T Park in conjunction with the San Francisco Giants. The idea was that consumers would use their mobile phones to take pictures of themselves or their friends using their Visa cards within the park. Then they sent us their photos via their mobile phones, and we posted them throughout the game on a jumbo screen.

It was really interesting for us to think about this program as a way to bring the Visa brand to a very specific group of cardholders within the confines of the park. It engaged consumers at a different level, while also supporting our underlying business strategy of having a Visa product be part of a transaction.

Zain Raj, Euro RSCG Chicago

It's a very ironic question that comes out of the old-world arrogance of traditional marketing. The fundamental belief has been that if you advertised your product, you could build a brand's identity through awareness alone. But that's never really been true.

A brand has never been anything but a relationship that consumers have with a product or service that fulfills a need in their lives. Consumers have always had the power to define what brands are going to stand for and what role the brand is going to play either in their lives or in the context of the marketplace.

If you think about it, one hundred years ago brands were built by consumers talking to one another. Today, the Internet and other technologies allow consumers to engage in that kind of conversation again, and the brands that succeed will be those that give them as much of an active role as they used to have.

Can You Hear Me Now?

Many marketers talk about having conversations with their customers, but few show anywhere near the dedication of a Tom Boyles, a Roger McGuinn, a Lisa Baird, or a *Mon Quotidien*.

Sure, they'll set up a blog, start an email newsletter, launch a viral video, or let their customers create their own commercials, as Heinz did. They might even let their customers customize their products, as Nike did with its now-famous Nike ID Web site and BMW did with its Mini Cooper design options, for example. These days, you can even customize the color of your M&Ms if you want to.

That's all great stuff, but there is so much more to it than that. What really matters is that it's the customer who is doing most of the talking, and the marketer is doing most of the listening. It is time to take a break, pick up the phone, and *listen*. Let your customers control the conversation and stop interrupting with all those irrelevant ads.

■ **Your brand's relevance is not about what you have to sell; it's about what your customers have to say.**

CHAPTER 5

Innovation

> When you're building a product that you're going to
> use yourself, you can be very good at marketing.
> —STEVE WOZNIAK

All Steve Wozniak really wanted to do was impress the other electronics freaks at the Homebrew Computer Club. It just so happened that one of those freaks was another Steve—Steve Jobs. It was the mid-1970s, and the two Steves actually had met before, in the summer of 1973, while Jobs and Woz (as he's popularly known) both worked at Hewlett-Packard.

From the start, Jobs knew he was not nearly the engineer that Woz was, but he believed he could parlay his friend's genius into a big idea. Woz wasn't so sure about that, but his friend turned out to be a pretty good salesman, and the Steves launched Apple Computer on April Fools' Day, 1976.

For a guy whom many credit with perhaps the pivotal role

in "inventing" the personal computer, Steve Wozniak is not very eager to take much credit. In fact, when I asked him if he thinks of himself as innovative, he paused and then said: "Gee, I don't know. Let me think about that. I don't know if I'd use that word, *innovative*." After another long pause, he decided that, yes, he was innovative, but it was clear that he didn't really think of himself that way. As he explained, "What I would do is look at the world and how other people were doing things. I just don't like conflict. I don't want to compete. I don't want to try to do the same thing better. So I went off in very different directions from what was obvious."

Of course, what wasn't obvious to others was as plain as day to Steve Wozniak, because his goal really wasn't to be innovative per se. His goal was to find practical solutions. "I always had a strong internal philosophy of trying to design things for normal, average people," he said. "More than that, I like to skip and jump to the spot needed and get straight to the point and do what's needed."

The idea of using a keyboard and a monitor with a computer is perhaps the most famous example of how Woz simply did what was needed:

Basically, I needed a keyboard to type programs in, and I needed output in the form of a video terminal. Input and output are the most expensive things. Output is by far the most expensive thing. I had to use the only output device I could think of, which was my home TV.

*So I built a terminal where I could type on a keyboard
and watch letters on my TV set and talk to a computer in
Boston via the Arpanet, which was the early Internet. All I
did was show it off to a few people . . . like Steve Jobs. And
he actually arranged for us to sell some.*

Yes, just a few! But becoming rich and famous as an inventor was not what Woz had in mind. He was mainly looking for a better way to test his work or play a game and have some fun. In fact, it was Woz's interest in games that led him to write the language for Apple in BASIC instead of FORTRAN, which was the scientific language.

"I had never programmed in BASIC in my life," said Woz, "but being able to program these games in BASIC told me that it was going to be the language that was going to be more popular."

When I spoke with Woz, I asked him if he ever found it hard to get along with marketing people. The question was really intended as a proxy for his sometimes contentious relationship with that master of marketing Steve Jobs, but Woz didn't take the hint.

"When we started Apple," said Woz, "Mike Markkula was funding us, and I respected him so much. He said that the top companies are marketing driven, not engineering driven. I totally bought into that. I worked alone, and I was marketing. When you're building a product that you're going to use yourself you can be very good at marketing."

Or, as Puma CEO Jochen Zeitz said in a 2002 interview with Reveries.com, "I think you have to live [innovation], ultimately. Words on paper don't mean anything. You have to live it yourself. Your whole management has to live it, and if you see any deviation, you have to step in and correct things."

■ **Relevant brands see themselves as their own best customers.**

Deere Prudence

At John Deere, CEO Robert Lane likes to remind people that "Deere was founded in 1837 after blacksmith John Deere invented a steel plow that worked well in prairie soil."

Robert hopes to continue in that tradition, reported Carol Hymowitz in the *Wall Street Journal*—to help its customers "work smarter and harder"—with innovations such as "new forestry equipment" that "allows operators to select and cut trees in a way that fosters regrowth."

Deere also formed an "Agri Services group, which is developing and marketing new services to help farmers grow more uniform crops," via a database of "three hundred thousand acres of cotton fields so farmers know precisely where to spray fertilizer." In another innovation, Deere's Agri Services "also aims to tell food companies and consumers more about what they're buying."

Dan McCabe, senior vice president of Deere Agri Services, explained, "We'll be able to trace exactly what's in the food we're eating, where it was grown, and what was done to it at every point in the food-production chain." The point is that "if a cereal company learns that certain crops make production easier or result in a better-tasting product, it may pay more for them."

Unfortunately, that level of commitment still tends to be the exception rather than the rule at most companies today. Thomas Kuczmarski of the Kellogg School at Northwestern University commented: "Executives have to define what they want to achieve, and give their strategy muscle and guts by allocating finances and their best talents."

Most of them still don't do that, apparently, but "with just-in-time inventory, outsourcing, and other cost-squeezing measures now widespread, executives know their companies must become more creative to capture customers in the global market."

■ **From simple steel plows to complex databases, John Deere's success in innovation is firmly rooted in its founder's focus on solving relevant problems.**

Innovation Versus Success

Despite its success—or maybe because of it—the National Football League is rarely thought of as innovative. Lisa Baird, when she was with the NFL, readily admitted that the League was not exactly a bastion of new ideas, but just as readily asserted that she was out to help change that.

Her greatest hurdle, she said, is a fear of failure. "In terms of innovation, our success is the hardest obstacle to overcome," said Lisa. "If you're in a successful company that has a successful business model, it's hard to create and go somewhere new because people are very afraid of disturbing that success."

Is innovation always critical to brand success? I put that question to Stephen Berkov, formerly of Audi and now with Edmunds.com, and he expressed some reservations: "I actually have a concern about the word *innovation* because there seems to be a lot of innovation for its own sake. Innovation is all about staying relevant. That's all it is. If you are losing relevance, you need to innovate. If you are perfectly relevant, there is less need to innovate."

Writing in the January 2007 issue of *The Hub*, Dr. Peter Temes, president of the ILO Institute, also noted a certain disconnect between those who advocate for innovation within organizations and the marketplace itself: "In the fourth quarter of 2006, the ILO Institute asked fifty senior executives at multibillion-dollar companies a series of questions about support for innovation inside and outside the companies, to establish a baseline for an annual innovation index. . . . With a score of 1.0 representing no change over one year ago, the overall average score was 1.41."

In other words, support for innovation among corporate executives was on the rise, at least in the categories surveyed by the ILO Institute. When the institute asked these executives to rate interest in innovation among their customers, however, the index fell to 1.275.

Peter concluded: "The gap between internal support for innovation and external marketplace realities might suggest problems ahead for companies that have adopted innovation as a theme without fully understanding or preparing for the inevitable high rate of new-product failures."

■ **Corporate enthusiasm for innovation is rising, but consumers don't always care.**

2100 Inventions

"Invention is really a systematic form of criticism," wrote Raymond F. Yates in his classic book *2100 Needed Inventions*, first published in 1942. As noted by Cynthia Crossen in the *Wall Street Journal*, Raymond's point was that we are most critical of the things that annoy us in everyday life, and these criticisms are the stuff of invention.

Raymond himself was critical of noisy things—lawnmowers, toilets, radiators, wooden floors, and bedsprings—and proposed that someone should invent something to silence them.

Raymond, who died in 1954 at the age of sixty-six, was also critical of his pipe and thought someone should invent a pipe that cleaned itself as you smoked it. Many of his suggested inventions were indeed rather frivolous, such as a banana peeler.

But, as Raymond observed, the real challenge of inventing wasn't invention, it was relevance. As evidence, Raymond pointed to the man who invented an electric rocking chair. What was the relevance of that?

Raymond's own top-ten list was a profile in relevance. His top three were "a way to transform energy with less waste, a more efficient way to store energy, and better light bulbs." He also envisioned "a personal television receiver that would fit into a vest pocket"; "a means by which the essence of tea or coffee can be crystallized so that it can be readily dissolved in hot water"; and "a safety match box that must be closed before the match can be struck."

■ **Relevance is the mother of invention.**

Nottingham-Spirk

Chances are that you have never heard of Nottingham-Spirk, the industrial-design firm whose creations include the Crest SpinBrush, the Dirt Devil vacuum cleaner, and the ever-popular Sherwin-Williams twist-and-pour paint can. In fact, over the past thirty years Nottingham-Spirk has "patented 464 products, with combined sales of more than $30 billion," according to Anne Fischer, writing in *Fortune*.

What's their secret? Craig Saunders, who has been with the firm for twenty-four years, said he simply asks consumers to talk about things that make them mad. That's how Nottingham-Spirk came up with the SwifferVac, for instance. Consumers thought the SwifferMop was great but were frustrated by its inability to clean up anything other than dust.

"So if you spilled cereal or dry dog food or jelly beans on the floor, you had to get out the vacuum cleaner. . . . People hated that," said Craig.

Another favorite research technique is simply to walk the aisles at Wal-Mart with an eye out for what's missing. That's how Nottingham-Spirk came up with the idea for the blockbuster Crest SpinBrush—just noticing how expensive electric toothbrushes were, how they were locked up in cases, and thinking how great it would be if you could just grab one for five bucks from the regular manual toothbrush rack and toss it in your shopping cart.

■ **Frustration is the mother of relevance.**

Return on Responsibility

You know him as Cool Hand Luke, Butch Cassidy, and, last but not least, the Salad Dressing Guy. But you may not know that actor Paul Newman is also an innovator in outsourcing—in a good way, of course.

The innovation is that everything Newman's Own markets is made by a third party; all of its quality assurance and research and development is outsourced, too. What is so innovative about that? As Tom Indoe, the company's president, told me, "You see a lot of major companies doing that today, but when Newman's started out . . . that degree of outsourcing wasn't done." The idea was to keep costs low while keeping quality high, and making sure there was as much money left over as possible to give to charities.

Tom said the concept is still going strong after more than two decades in business. "Our net profits are equal to or better than most food companies," he reported. Not only that, but the film star's contributions have totaled more than $200 million over the past twenty-plus years.

What would happen if more marketers stopped obsessing over gaining incremental advantages through the analysis of their marketing expenditures and began wrapping their heads around the connection between altruism and innovation? They just might find their way to a different kind of ROI—where the "I" stands for innovation and the return is on responsibility.

■ **Newman's Own is a great example of the sometimes strong link between innovation and altruism.**

Sustainable Guitars

For those in the business of building guitars, sustainable design isn't a marketing gimmick; in fact, it is just the opposite. The problem, as reported by Glenn Rifkin in the *New York Times*, is that most musicians want guitars made of Sitka spruce, mahogany, ebony, and rosewood—endangered old-growth timber that not only makes guitars look the way guitars are supposed to look but, more important, creates the finest sounding guitars.

Sure, alternative woods are available, but they generally don't look or sound great. So for guitar makers like Martin, Gibson, and Taylor, "green marketing" by itself is kind of a nonstarter. They need to find a way to continue to build the kinds of guitars their customers want.

But what a dilemma. "If I use up all the good wood, I'm out of business," said Chris Martin, the sixth-generation CEO of C. F. Martin & Company. "I have a two-year-old daughter, Claire Frances Martin, and she can be the seventh generation C. F. Martin. I want her to be able to get materials she'll need, just as my ancestors and I have over the past 174 years."

Most troubling to Chris and his competitors is the clear-cutting of Sitka spruce, "a tonal wood used for the soundboards of acoustic guitars. . . . To achieve the sound that guitarists cherish, the Sitka spruce, at least 250 years old, has long been a required material."

The thing is that guitar makers use only "a tiny fraction" of the Sitka spruce that is shipped; the entire guitar-building industry needs only about 150 logs per year. About 80 percent of the wood is shipped to Japan and is used to build homes. It actually was Greenpeace that figured this out after checking the records of a large logging company called Sealaska. Greenpeace then enlisted Chris and his competitors to join the effort to protect old-growth forests through better management.

Chris said he doesn't want to tell others how to run their businesses, but he doesn't want shortsighted economic goals to endanger the future of his own business. He commented, "None of us wants to cut the last tree."

- **Sustaining relevance can require a kind of innovation in reverse—that is, finding new ways to continue doing things the way they've always been done.**

Killer Kleenex

"It could alter people's perceptions of what a Kleenex facial tissue could do," said Steve Erb, a Kleenex marketing director, recalling the 2004 launch of a new kind of facial tissue infused with pesticides, as reported by Ellen Byron in the *Wall Street Journal*.

Kleenex had come a long way since its 1924 introduction "as a handy way for women to remove cold cream from their faces." In the 1930s it was repositioned "as a disposable handkerchief." In 1967 it became something of a fashion statement with the introduction of "cube-shaped boxes," and in 1981 "Kleenex pioneered the first perfumed tissue with a light floral scent." Somewhere along the way Kleenex became the Google of facial tissues.

By the turn of the twenty-first century, however, Kleenex was casting about for a new point of relevance. Consumers were increasingly using "paper towels, toilet paper, and free napkins available at coffeeshops and fast-food chains" instead of Kleenex. "Advances in cold therapies" also contributed to sales declines. So in 2004, Kimberly-Clark, makers of Kleenex, decided it needed to promote a facial tissue that could also kill germs. The idea held promise because "74 percent of consumers" had the "yucky habit" of stashing and reusing tissues.

It actually was not the first time Kleenex tried this, having introduced, and subsequently withdrawn, a germ-fighting tissue called Avert Virucidal back in the mid-1980s. Kleenex figured it could get it right this time with a better name, a better package, and the claim that the new tissue's "middle layer traps and kills 99.9 percent of viruses within 15 minutes." And despite some concern about balancing the brand's gentle image with deadly properties, it launched Kleenex Anti-Viral using the ad tagline: "Ruthless Killer."

The bottom line is that two years later the product was a success, having claimed 4 percent of the U.S. market and $140 million in global sales across twenty-two countries.

- **Kleenex sustained relevance for more than eighty years by changing its positioning from "fashion" to "utility" to "necessity."**

Aga Cookers

Having "remained virtually unchanged since 1922, Aga proved that even the stodgiest brands could strike a lucrative balance between tradition and innovation," reported Elizabeth Esfahani in *Business 2.0.*

Aga is "a half-ton cooker" (that would be a "range" here in America). It is well known in the United Kingdom as "a symbol of Britain's stuffy fox-hunting set." It has actually been around for more than eighty years and has even "spawned a genre of fiction," known as "Aga sagas," featuring "Britain's country-dwelling upper middle class." But backed by a $2 million marketing campaign, it became a "totem of hip modern design."

The ad campaign positioned the Aga "as a central part of a kitchen makeover" but also played up the one thing that has always made Aga radically different: "Aga's cooker is always on, eschewing knobs and controls in favor of compartments that are constantly heated at different temperatures."

Aga's salespeople assure skeptical customers that keeping the heat on at all times "has a negligible effect on energy bills. . . . Some Aga owners have found innovative uses for the heat, like warming up on chilly days, drying clothes, and, in the case of one customer, using the 150-degree compartment to hatch ostrich eggs."

This careful combination of legacy design and new features paid off for Aga. In 2006 "revenues swelled 15 percent to $501 million, while profit was up 16 percent to $43 million."

■ **Aga's innovation was a reintroduction of its old-fashioned features, rejuvenating its relevance among a younger generation of consumers.**

Chip Control

Line extensions are a way of life for consumer packaged goods companies, but "product proliferation is rarely successful," wrote Cameron Stracher in the *Wall Street Journal*. It is easy to see why manufacturers think that if some is good, more is better. For one thing, offering more flavors, colors, shapes, or sizes of the same product enables them to play with price points, "selling more popular items for a higher price and trying to 'trade up' consumers to 'premium' products. Extending an existing line is also a lot cheaper than developing and marketing a new product."

Besides, the factory is pretty much already set up for it, and there is also the promise of more shelf space—a veritable billboard of your brand in all its glorious varieties. But there are limits, of course, as pointed out by John Quelch and David Kenny "in their seminal paper on the subject." Specifically, "extending a brand almost always results in cannibalizing sales from the original. There's a limit to how much toothpaste we can use, for example, and buying Crest Tartar Protection Whitening Cool Mint Paste will most likely take sales from Crest Whitening Plus Scope Extreme Mint Explosion rather than from Colgate."

The tragedy is that what the shopper most likely wanted

was plain old Crest, and it's hard to find amid all the other varieties. So not only are shoppers deprived of what they wanted, but the brand has spent more money on ensuring their frustration. Crest may or may not be succeeding with this strategy, but in most cases the scenario leads to depressed profits and newly disloyal shoppers trying something else.

The point is that Diet Coke, for example, may satisfy those who wish for something brown and bubbly but without the calories, but few people "wish they could eat potato chips if only there were a yogurt and green onion variety."

■ **In their quest to innovate, companies often fail to understand that these innovations have to be worth trying.**

Less Is More

For some unknown reason, A. G. Lafley wouldn't come to the phone when I called to ask about his insights on innovation. Equally inexplicably, the P&G CEO instead took a call from Geoffrey Colvin of *Fortune*—and even sat down for a face-to-face interview to share what he knows. Geoffrey's excellent Q&A was published in the December 11, 2006, edition of *Fortune*. Because innovation came up during Geoffrey's interview, I thought we should highlight some of A.G.'s comments here. No hard feelings.

One key to innovation, said A.G., is focus. "I don't know how it happens, but in every case I've been associated with over almost thirty years, the focus gets diffused. More projects get started than anybody can manage." So at P&G the focus "is on just eight to ten core technologies where we want to be world class," he explained. The idea that less can be more when it comes to innovation is just one part of A.G.'s strategy, but it certainly is a key to Procter & Gamble's growth. For at least five years running, A.G. said, P&G clocked in at 6 percent annual organic growth (that means excluding acquisitions), on average.

A.G.'s approach is somewhat similar to that of John Pepper, his predecessor as CEO at Procter & Gamble. In his book *What Really Matters*, John recalled how a singular focus on one idea—even one *word*—was essential to the success of Dawn dishwashing detergent when it was first introduced in 1972. That word was *grease*, and the idea was that Dawn was better at removing it than competing brands. At the time, conventional wisdom was that so much emphasis on just one brand could be limiting. Well, it wasn't—at least until Colgate-Palmolive came along with a fresh range of fragrances and packaging, forcing Dawn to expand its focus a little bit to remain competitive.

Procter & Gamble's focus on innovation is consistent with the philosophy espoused by Michael George, coauthor of a 2005 book called *Fast Innovation*. In a *Wall Street Journal* article by George Anders, Michael said that the hardest part of making innovation happen is convincing "scientists, design-ers, or other creative types" to put *fewer* ideas into the pipeline. To make his point, Michael offered this analogy: "If a freeway is getting congested, do you load more cars onto the on-ramp in hopes that people will go faster? Or should you try to take some cars off?"

Michael's perspective is based on "queueing theory," an ap-proach commonly used by factory managers to avoid bottle-necks. The idea is to "keep a little slack in the system to handle the unpredictable—but inevitable—crunch times." Michael's advice appeared to work well for Avery Dennison Corp., which had become "vexed . . . at how long it took to turn ideas into products." By reducing the amount of "slack time," Avery was able "to ensure that critical tasks stayed on schedule."

Avery's Tim Bond commented: "Instead of killing ourselves on too many projects, we think we're able to move a smaller number through the system more rapidly." He added, "So now we ask ourselves on each project, what's the effort-to-benefit trade-off. . . . We don't want to have a few marginal projects stop us from doing our best on the big ones."

"Less is more" also pretty much summed up Nike's growth strategy, as reported by Stephanie Kang in the *Wall Street Jour-nal*. "They're realizing they don't need ten to fifteen kinds of Jordan shoes," said Robert Samuels, a J. P. Morgan analyst. "They're really focusing on those things that are selling."

Most notably, Nike brought a fresh focus to the humble T-shirt, as part of a new collection called Sports Essentials. In the past,

Nike had thirty different T-shirt designs, but the new strategy called for just one design. It came in ten colors, however, twice the usual palette. Nike's Roger Wyett commented, "What we're looking to do is evolve into a predictable business that's driven by key styles." If all goes as planned, Nike will reach "$23 billion in revenue by 2011—a boost of 54 percent from this year—by focusing on fewer, high-return opportunities."

Burberry's took a similar track—that is, putting a narrower focus on what sold best, according to a *Wall Street Journal* article by Cecilie Rohwedder. For Burberry's, part of that plan was to return to its iconic trench coat, which had become a symbol of its past. Now you can get a trench coat done up in sequins, alligator, or mink—or as dresses and capes. Overall, Burberry's reduced its total number of products by a third, to about forty-two hundred styles a year instead of six thousand. With polo shirts, for example, Burberry's jettisoned six of its twenty styles. Burberry's also revised its delivery schedule (shipping five small collections a year instead of two big ones) and made sure that what was showing in its window displays was the same as what was featured in its advertising.

Initial results were pretty good, sending Burberry's sales up 14 percent versus the previous year and putting its stock on an upward trajectory, too.

■ **If some is good, more isn't necessarily better.**
  A disciplined focus on what matters most is essential
  to innovation and growth.

Encouraging Innovation

How do you encourage people to be innovative? I asked some successful motivators at Colgate-Palmolive, Best Buy, Audi, and Squidoo.com.

Jim Figura, Colgate-Palmolive

In general, Colgate allows people to pursue things that they find of interest and that they feel could influence the course of the business. But we've also done a number of things that are more formalized.

One good example is a company-wide program that was initiated two years ago called "Innovation Everywhere." It encourages Colgate employees to find new ways to solve old problems or bring in tools to help with the commercial process of the company.

To support that effort, the company started a global innovation fund, which provides seed money to employees who submit ideas. The ideas are then judged by a group of executives covering a broad cross-functional range of the company.

It is not just about marketing and new products, it's really every function in the company that participates. Well over one hundred projects have been funded so far.

Mike Linton, formerly of Best Buy (currently of eBay)

At Best Buy, the whole team—people in the media department, brand group, or market research department—would get credit for innovating outside their space. We didn't want money and people to become locked up in their current work. It is usually culture or people, versus some perfect kind of operating system, that produce innovations.

We would always try to do something new every year—new in terms of its impact on the marketplace. We would always dedicate some money and some people—not a ton, but some—to trying new things. If you don't do that, money for innovation is almost always the first to be taken away in a budget crunch because it doesn't have any immediate impact.

Stephen Berkov, formerly of Audi (currently of Edmunds.com)

Each person on the team needs to bring exactly who they are to the table and not hide that. It's the job of the director, or the person who is orchestrating, to bring the team together in a dynamic way.

The brand is the guiding light, and we are its ambassadors. It is actually not that difficult if we know what our brand is—its DNA, its values, its personality—and why it deserves a place in the market. Then each person on the team brings unique talents to help make it happen.

Seth Godin, Squidoo.com

Most organizations, big and small, are lying to themselves at the most senior levels. They are pretending that they want innovation, but they really don't. The number-one way to get your people to be innovative is to welcome the innovations that they've already accomplished and to do something about them.

Most organizations that are stuck have plenty of innovation floating around that people are trying to pitch but that never goes anywhere. As soon as you accept the fact that your people are smart—and do something about it—you'll discover that they will continue to innovate.

Innovation Farms

When it comes to innovation, Judith L. Estrin thinks it's helpful for big companies to think of themselves as farms, as reported by Scott Thurm in the *Wall Street Journal*. Judith made the comment in response to a question about how to "get people to think beyond eighteen months if the whole company is focused on eighteen months." This was her response:

> *In thinking about large companies, think of them as farms. And what you're trying to do is grow rows of corn. You don't want surprises, you want it to work well; you apply incremental innovation to be as productive as you can.*
>
> *And then when you're thinking about start-ups or disruptive innovation, think about that as either a greenhouse or maybe a small garden plot where surprises are fun. All of a sudden you look out into your garden, and there's something out there that makes it look better and it is interesting.*

You have a different level of nurturing that you need for a small garden. Then the greenhouse is a step further, where you really want to control the conditions and keep out the elements. So, I think what we have seen as the most disruptive innovation has come from start-up and research, because they naturally operate in that fashion with a clean slate.

Or you can decide to develop greenhouses and small garden plots on the farm. But you have to keep them separate, and then the trick is transplanting. And I'm not a gardener, even though I use this analogy, but transplanting is the trickiest part of growing things. And so you really have to build in a culture and figure out for your organization, how are the best ways to transplant? Do you move people? How much do you let the business grow before you transplant it, how do you prepare the soil?

Judith, who is CEO of Packet Design, Inc., also advised that "you can't measure innovation in process." Or—if she were to extend the analogy—don't pull innovation up from its roots to check its growth.

The Dream Factory

What began in June 1984 as a not-for-profit enterprise featuring a nomadic troupe of street artists led by founder Guy Laliberte evolved into Cirque du Soleil, a global sensation driven by more than thirty-eight hundred employees, deploying as many as fifteen separate handcrafted shows worldwide.

Mario D'Amico is one of those employees, having joined Cirque du Soleil in 1999 as its chief marketing officer after a long career in the advertising agency business. I asked Mario about the difference between working in an ad agency and Cirque. This was his response:

> It is actually incredibly different, and in fact I'm shocked every day at how different it is. Here the creators that create are really true artists in the sense that they are not necessarily thinking of an audience when they're creating. They are just expressing themselves, their emotions, their angst, their preoccupations, and their worries. They are creating for themselves. That there is a public out there that's willing to buy a ticket and come see the result of that creative effort is almost secondary.
>
> The way the creative teams work is a very introverted process. That's very different from the process in the ad agency world. Creative people at agencies are creating with a client in mind, usually, with a budget in mind, and definitely with a target audience in mind. It couldn't be more different here at Cirque.

The difference is also evident in Cirque du Soleil's working environment. Two huge training gyms, each the size of a small airplane hangar, are smack in the center of company headquarters. So if you're an accountant or a marketing person sitting at your desk, you have this huge window in front of you through which you can watch your coworkers practicing maybe a Russian swing act while you're working on your budgets.

As Mario described it, "You'll see people in tights walking by, next to graphics people, next to accountants, next to IT people, and it just really looks like one of these 'we are the world' type of places! So it's really exciting."

■ **Cirque du Soleil's innovations may be a result of artists simply expressing themselves, but its relevance may be a result of the "tights" mixing with the "suits."**

Born-Again Virgin

Tower Records went out of business, and much of the rest of the record industry went flat on its back. But it was quite a different story at Virgin Megastores in North America where marketing chief Dee Mc Laughlin fills the room with the ring of success.

"Our stats are through the roof, double digits every day," she told me in late 2007. "Board meetings are very happy occasions. . . . We just keep pushing on through."

It's true. As of late December 2007, Virgin's same-store sales were up a remarkable 14 percent for the year, gaining sales at nearly the same rate that the record business was losing sales. How is that possible? Dee Mc Laughlin explained it in just four syllables: Innovation.

"It literally is that simple," said Dee. "It's about coming up with easier ways to give our customers what they want." And that, she said, is also pretty simple. "We observe, and then we innovate." For example, Virgin observed that their shoppers were confused by the differences between HD and Blu-ray video formats, so they installed an HD and Blu-ray wall in all of their stores.

"Where before we had consumer confusion, which was potentially stifling sales of both systems, now our customers actually can see what the difference is and choose for themselves which format to buy," Dee explained. "I really feel that a lot of the time retailers can miss the simplest things. So it is all about what did I miss or what didn't I observe?" Of course it helps if your boss is Sir Richard Branson. "What's great about Virgin," said Dee, "is that the sky's the limit. In fact, it's not even the limit anymore because we have Virgin Galactic now. We don't even have a ceiling on this brand anymore!"

■ **Virgin sailed where others sank because of a simple two-step approach to innovation: observing its shoppers and then developing relevant solutions.**

Starwood Six Sigma

Starwood Hotels combined its "culture of creativity" with the discipline of Six Sigma, fostering innovations that in 2006 "delivered more than $100 million in profits to its bottom line," reported Spencer E. Ante in *BusinessWeek*.

"We have been driving our margin growth faster than our competitors. . . . When people ask why, I point to Six Sigma," said Geoffrey A. Ballotti, president of Starwood N.A. Starwood initiated the approach back in 2001, which involved training "150 employees as 'black belts' and more than 2,700 'green belts' in the arts of Six Sigma." The "black belts" supervise projects, and "green belts" sweat the details.

The ideas for the projects themselves, however, "come from in-house staff." For example, "after a study found that 34 percent of frequent travelers feel lonely away from home," Starwood's Westin Chicago River North hotel initiated a project called "Unwind." Its purpose was "to think up a set of nightly activities that would draw guests out of their rooms and into the lobby where they could mingle, develop a greater loyalty to the hotel group, and maybe spend a little more money."

During a brainstorming session with Starwood's black belts and green belts, the hotel's fitness director came up with the idea of offering massages. The Six Sigma team liked the idea and figured out how to make it work as efficiently as possible. Starwood knew the idea was working because it uses "a proprietary Web-based system . . . to monitor a slew of performance metrics to gauge the success or failure of a new project."

As of 2007 the system contained some three thousand to four thousand items—the "Unwind" program itself has spawned 120 ideas—"one for each of Starwood's hotels, including traditional fire dancing in Fiji and Chinese watercolor painting in Beijing."

Geoffrey Ballotti said he was pleased with the team effort: "I probably will make 50 percent fewer mistakes than if I had rolled out a project myself," he said.

■ **Starwood Hotels put relevance at the center of its innovation process and was able to quantify the bottom-line results.**

Innovation Versus Creativity

The thing about innovation is that, like creativity, it is widely considered to be mysterious. Some people think that if you try to deconstruct creativity, you will destroy it in the process.

But unlike creativity, innovation is all about practicality, about solving problems and making things work. Creativity only needs to be clever. So, in many ways, innovation sets a higher standard than mere creativity, but it is also much simpler and much less mysterious. That doesn't stop us from ascribing a certain mystery to innovation, most commonly by repeating the myth that innovators are somehow different from the rest of us—that they are, in fact, misfits.

Bill Gates legendarily dropped out of college to start Microsoft (of course, the college he dropped out of was, um, Harvard). Steve Wozniak fits a similar archetype as quirky outsider who accidentally changed the world. Those are both such great stories. However, David A. Hollinger, a historian, thinks we should stop feeding such legends. "The celebration of misfits promotes a worrisome anti-intellectualism and presents a distorted picture of the innovation process," he said in a *New York Times* column by G. Pascal Zachary.

His point was that guys like Gates and Wozniak are far from typical and that most innovation happens as "a result of large teams working in routine, predictable ways." He may be right, but whether or not misfits dominate innovation is irrelevant. What is important is the understanding that innovation is about solving problems, often in ostensibly mundane incremental ways.

Steve Wozniak needed a monitor so he could see what he was typing, and he figured out how to hook up a TV set to his computer. He said keyboards had been used with computers before, and he simply figured out a way to make them work on a small scale, for individual users. There is really nothing very mysterious about what Woz did, and it's not very different from other famous innovations. For example, contrary to popular belief, James Watt did not invent the steam engine, Eli Whitney didn't invent the cotton gin, and Robert Fulton did not invent the steamboat. All three of those inventions actually were incremental or derivative improvements on existing technologies.

In his book *A Culture of Improvement*, Robert Friedel noted that these and other inventions typically were "preceded by similar machines that incorporated most, if not all, of the principles of the famous devices." His main point, as cited in a *Wall Street Journal* book review by Adam Keiper, was this: "Too often the existence of a key patent or the success of a manufacturing enterprise has diverted attention from the long and gradual history of creativity."

That history, he argues, is not about "advancing human reason or a great impersonal force directing the course of history. Rather, it proceeds by fits and starts—held back, pushed forward, or diverted by social and biographical contingencies." For example, Robert Fulton's name is forever associated with the steamboat not because he "invented" it but because he had the "capitalist vision and fortitude" to figure out how to make money from it. In other words, he was kind of like Steve Wozniak and Steve Jobs all rolled into one!

■ **Any misfit can come up with a creative idea, but if it doesn't work, it's not relevant. And if it's not relevant, it's not innovative.**

CHAPTER 6

Investment

Spare No Expense

There's always someone who will say that you could sell
just as much without spending the extra money.
—Donna Sturgess

Donna Sturgess found herself up against those who
never saw a cost they wouldn't cut as she and her team
developed Aquafresh Extreme Clean, a new entry in
the ostensibly mundane toothpaste category. "The cost-of-goods
conversation is always a challenge," she said with a sigh when I
interviewed her in the spring of 2006.

Donna knew that success depended on creating a different
kind of toothpaste—one that would provide a decidedly different experience versus Colgate and Crest, the category's leaders. As the third-place player, Aquafresh was in a bind. If the
brand didn't start to sell better, it was in danger of losing its
relevance in the marketplace altogether. Reasserting its rele-

vance started with the toothpaste itself. Finding a flavor that wasn't mint and a formula that created more foaming action may not have cost anything extra (or at least was not necessarily the kind of expense that would come under immediate scrutiny). Engaging engineers to design a cap that closes with a click (instead of the usual flip top or screw cap), however, started to push things.

When Donna insisted that the carton be made of plastic instead of paper (so that it would stand out in stores while also building more excitement and loyalty among consumers), she really had to fight for it. She commented, "There's always internal tension over 'Why can't you do it cheaper?' This product went through as much rigor as any new product launch, with a bit more challenge around some things that you can certainly tell cost more money. But the result is that Extreme Clean put the brand back onto a growth trajectory."

Donna's success story would certainly seem to be an exception rather than a rule in today's marketplace, where most brands are obsessed with cutting costs and infatuated with measuring each incremental expense against each incremental return on investment.

- **What is relevant to consumers can be different from what is relevant to numbers crunchers.**

Play It Again, Ringo

One wouldn't think that cost control was ever an issue for the Beatles, especially when they were recording the *Sgt. Pepper* album at the height of their fame. But, in fact, the subject of costs and budgets apparently arose frequently whenever John Lennon or Paul McCartney wanted to do something a little bit crazy.

As Geoff Emerick, the group's recording engineer, recounts in his memoir, *Here, There and Everywhere*, the matter of expense nearly squashed John Lennon's request to hire a ninety-piece orchestra to fill a twenty-four-bar gap in one of his songs, "A Day in the Life." John thought it would be really cool to have London's finest classical musicians show up and simply play every note on their instruments, from the highest to the lowest, each at his or her own pace, without a conductor.

George Martin, the Beatles' producer, was no doubt horrified at the thought of asking these classically trained musicians—many of whom were his personal friends—to do such a thing, purely from an artistic perspective. However, his pushback was not artistic but economic; he simply told John that EMI, the Beatles' record company, wouldn't pay for a full orchestra to play just twenty-four bars. It didn't matter that at the time the Beatles were the most profitable property on EMI's roster or even in the world. From the record company's point of view, *Sgt. Pepper* would sell just as many copies with or without hiring a full orchestra for the sake of twenty-four bars on one song.

Maybe the Fab Four's relevance wasn't exactly at stake

here—unless you consider their reputation for insanely great experimentation an element of their relevance in popular culture. The band probably thought so. John was flummoxed, but Ringo Starr provided a solution: Why not bring in half an orchestra and have them play twice? So that's what they did. The rest, as they say, is psychedelic history.

The Price of Relevance

Intelligentsia Coffee carved out relevance for itself by paying coffee growers a premium based on the quality of their crops.

"Intelligentsia was known as this stupid and naive company that overpaid farmers and carried too much debt," Peter Giuliano of Counter Culture Coffee told Michaele Weissman of the *New York Times*. Notice that Peter was speaking in the past tense. Intelligentsia Coffee might have paid "at least 25 percent above the Fair Trade price" for its coffee, but it turned a profit, "with 2005 sales of $9.4 million and a 2006 growth rate of 21 percent."

Intelligentsia's key to success was the idea that drinkers would pay considerably more for better quality coffee and that growers could share in the margins if they produced better beans. Intelligentsia's idea apparently took notions of Fair Trade to another level—that is, not only as it relates to working conditions but also as it relates to the quality of the product itself.

Traditionally, growers are paid about the same for their crops regardless of quality, even though it is much harder work to grow quality beans. Their return is only what the co-op will bear, and that's pretty much the same for everybody. Intelligentsia's founders, Geoff Watts and Doug Zell, basically offered an incentive program that was premised on creating a relationship with farmers and not just completing a transaction. They set up a rating system called a "cupping score," modeled on the way estate wines are evaluated.

Intelligentsia paid "$1.60 a pound for AA coffee that earned a cupping score of 84 to 87 (on a scale of 100); $1.85 a pound for AAA coffees that earned scores of 88 to 93; and an unheard-of $3.00 a pound for extraordinary coffee that scored 94 and above."

By comparison, Fair Trade coffee typically sold for about "$1.26 for a pound of nonorganic beans and $1.41 for organic. Intelligentsia's prices would never go down; they would only go up, Intelligentsia promised. Local co-ops were simply paid a flat fee of about 26 cents per pound for services such as "dry-milling the beans, prefinancing the crop, and providing technical assistance."

The growers, meanwhile, were put in charge of judging their own beans, using Intelligentsia's standards. Geoff Watts called the approach "relationship coffee" and said he expected "to pay 50 percent, 100 percent, even 200 percent above Fair Trade rates for beans that were so good that customers would pay $20 and more a pound retail." He commented, "On the grower side and the consumer side, we're trying to create a culture of quality."

■ **By building a business model that was more relevant
to its suppliers, Intelligentsia created a product that
was so relevant to consumers that they paid a premium
for it.**

Rich Niche

EV Rental Cars found a profitable relevance in renting hybrid
cars even though it meant paying full retail prices for the autos
it rented. The big car rental companies wouldn't dream of doing such a thing because their business models were premised
on buying fleets based on volume discounts.

For the Hertzes and the Enterprises of the world, the problem was partly that the hybrid supply just wasn't big enough,
reported Gwendolyn Bounds in the *Wall Street Journal.* If you
have a fleet of 650,000 like Enterprise, having "about fifty hybrids" made it tough to promote their availability to consumers. "Manufacturers aren't making them available to us," said
Enterprise spokesperson Christy Conrad, who also noted that
consumer demand was there for hybrids. Cost is another problem because "while most car-rental companies bought vehicles
at a volume discount, EV paid manufacturers' suggested retail
prices."

EV could afford to do that in part "because of grants it has
received from the Transportation Department to educate consumers about alternative-energy cars." In fact, "with more

consumers considering hybrid purchases, renting was a way to get an extended test-drive first," EV founder Jeff Pink pointed out. Paying full retail for its cars also worked out for EV because "the aftermarket for hybrids was so robust it often could sell one of its used Priuses and then turn around and buy a new one for just a few hundred dollars more."

According to Jeff Pink, "EV was profitable in 2005 based on revenues of $4 million and projected revenues of $5 million to $6 million in 2006." And EV's "average monthly utilization rate"—that is, the number of days a car generates revenues—stood at 90 percent compared to an industry average of 80 to 85 percent, according to Abrams Consulting Group.

■ **EV Rental Cars found its edge against much bigger competitors by investing heavily in a highly relevant niche.**

Tardy Atari

A few big-name brands seem to be catching the spare-no-expense bug, too. Atari, for example, turned its excessive ways into part of its marketing strategy. In fact, Atari's vice president of sales and marketing, Nique Fajors, actually bragged to the *New York Times* about how late he was with the introduction of Test Drive Unlimited, an online racing simulation video game created for Microsoft's Xbox 360 console.

He told the *Times*: "From a product quality standpoint, you should know that we have delayed the game four times." While he said Atari would have loved to have launched the new game sooner to get some revenues going, he explained that "the viewpoint is that we will ship it when it's ready and not before, which is what is done for all the truly great products."

Test Drive Unlimited's level of sophistication was said to be a first for Xbox and certainly for Atari, whose reputation had tended to be defined by "cheap B-list games often thinly derived from tired licenses like the *Matrix* film series."

Atari actually began its production process with Eden Games in 2003, with a budget said to be "between $15 million and $25 million," give or take $10 million. And Microsoft, which would earn a royalty on each sale, saw Test Drive Unlimited as a good example of how to get video games right: "It isn't about just selling a $50 or $60 product at retail anymore," said John Smith of Microsoft. "It's about how you also keep people engaged with your title over time, and that means online content."

- **Atari bet that taking the long road would give it a much-needed point of relevance.**

Heineken Heights

Heineken spent fifteen months testing twenty different versions of a light beer before coming up with a brew with "a pale amber color and a crisp taste" that played to "the strengths of its core lager brand, which had a full flavor and a rich tawny color," reported Adrienne Carter in *BusinessWeek*. Then there was the matter of the bottle: "Its green glass and short neck are pure Heineken. And a slimmer, taller silhouette gives it a modern minimalist look." Such attention to detail paid off for Heineken.

Once they converted, consumers were paying about 50 cents more per bottle in a bar or restaurant versus Bud Light. Perhaps best of all for Heineken, sales of Premium Light appeared to lift sales of its flagship brand. Heineken said it expected its Premium Light sales to double again, to more than one million barrels, in 2007.

■ **Expensive attention to the details paid off for Heineken.**

Toyota Recall

Toyota paid any price and carried any burden to ensure that its customers were happy with its cars. Their strategy centered on issuing vehicle recalls early and often—typically before consumers even knew there was a problem at all, reported Joann Muller and Jonathan Fahey in *Forbes*.

Toyota had the auto industry's second-highest number of recalls in 2005, but it also dominated consumer satisfaction polls by J. D. Power. Only Ford, with 11.7 percent of its vehicles recalled in 2005, exceeded Toyota, which recalled 10.1 percent, followed by GM at 6.8 percent, Honda at 4 percent, and Chrysler at 2.5 percent.

During May 2006 alone, Toyota recalled "one million vehicles worldwide." And yet Toyota's cars sold rapidly because consumers were sold on their quality. Chance Power of J. D. Power observed: "What we tend to see is that if a customer receives a recall notice before their car exhibits any symptoms, they don't see it as a problem." In addition, Toyota gave its dealers "plenty of leeway to fix customer complaints even post-warranty—by some accounts as much as $3,000 per vehicle." And yet the amount Toyota spent on honoring warranties was "just 1.2 percent of revenues versus 2.4 percent for GM and 2.3 percent for Ford."

The high number of recalls was also because Toyota is so efficient, sharing parts across a number of models. As a result, when there is a problem, it means the recall applies to a large number of vehicles.

- **It seems counterintuitive to issue large numbers of product recalls—and it is certainly expensive—but for Toyota it underscored the supremely relevant issue of product quality.**

BMW Flexibility

Toyota may have had a lock on efficiency, but BMW found its edge in flexibility, reported Peter Gumbel in *Time*. "It's a flexibility that affects almost everything the firm touches, from the layout of its assembly lines to the working hours of its administrative staff to relationships with its unions and key suppliers," he wrote. As a result, "BMW . . . mastered the manufacturing fine art called mass customization: No two cars rolling through its assembly lines on any given day are identical." It is a flexibility that not only enables BMW's customers to change their minds about options up until six days before their cars go into production, but also fattens BMW's profits.

It seems that those who buy BMWs change their minds about what they want—a lot. In fact, according to BMW, "customers change their orders more than one million times a year. BMW doesn't break out details of the additional revenue, but given the profit margins on many add-ons," the flexibility pays off because the changes almost invariably are upgrades, not cutbacks. Such flexibility does mean that BMW can't produce as many cars per day as does Toyota, but as auto industry expert Garel Rhys points out, "BMW is not prepared to sacrifice its ability to give consumers the car they want. The alternative would be reduced costs but not the ability to charge a premium for customized cars."

"It is all about mastering complexity," said BMW CEO Norbert Reithofer. For starters, BMW's plant "is set up to handle five or six different BMW models simultaneously," and BMW "juggles some three hundred working-time permutations" to optimize its flexibility. What is more, "production processes can be added to the assembly line at any time without disrupting the work flow," and "several key suppliers are based in the plant," enabling them to customize solutions on the spot.

Toyota may still be the biggest and most profitable automaker, but Norbert Reithofer suggested that his "product-driven" approach was likely to prevail over Toyota's "process-driven" style over time. BMW sold "nearly 1.4 million cars in 2006, bringing in $65 billion in revenue."

■ **Giving consumers exactly what they want—even when they change their minds—isn't cheap or easy, but it is profitable for BMW.**

Seafood Stew

About five years ago, Stew Leonard Jr. and Fred Papp did something that almost never happens in a supermarket: They tore down the old seafood department in Stew's Norwalk, Connecticut, store and built a new one. It almost never happens because it is both expensive and disruptive. But Fred was lucky because Stew was prepared to spend what was required.

"Stew knew the big picture," Fred told me. "He wanted the

seafood department to be a destination for the store. He understood that people will drive a good distance to get to a quality fresh seafood market." Just as important, Fred explained, many shoppers judge the rest of the store by the seafood department. They figure that if the seafood is fresh, then everything else must be, too.

The transition period was anything but easy, with Fred and his team selling fish out of buckets of ice from a makeshift platform for about six months. But when the new department was unveiled, it was a stunner—all stainless steel and German glass, clean, industrial, and modern while still maintaining a certain classic fish counter quality about it. Best of all, said Fred, the new design put the "show and sell" of the seafood department front and center. Previously, all the preparation was done in a back room, out of view. Now shoppers can watch as Fred and his crew slice, fillet, bone, and otherwise dress the seafood for sale.

The effect of this is not limited to just shoppers, either. It extends to Fred's suppliers and his staff, too. "When really big seafood vendors come in and have not seen our bar before, their jaws drop because nobody in their right mind is going to have twenty-six different kinds of fresh fish on display the way we do," said Fred. The most you might normally see is maybe twelve or fifteen kinds of fish.

The new format also enables his staff to alternate easily between prepping fish and serving customers, adding a whole new level of efficiency to the operation. "The staff is working together better, and they're definitely happier because they all took some part in designing the department and are really proud of it," said Fred. His boss is happy, too. "Stew enjoys a good fish, wants other people to enjoy it, and knew that if we built a nice place to buy great fish, it would pay off." And it did.

■ **Sparing no expense can be just as much about disrupting normal operations and risking profits as it is about spending money.**

Working Backward

If there were a crown for spending more to make more, it would probably rest on the head of Gamal Aziz of the MGM Grand Casino. Gamal created a process he calls "working backward," as reported by Paula Kihla in *Business 2.0.* The process effectively shifted the focus from how much money was being made to how much *could* be made.

"If I listened to Six Sigma, . . . I'd be sitting here five years later measuring things," said Gamal Aziz, explaining why he prefers to tear things apart to build them back up.

Unlike Six Sigma, which "stresses improving current product by removing defects," Gamal's approach started from a decidedly loftier premise. He "breaks down an operation into constituent parts, then calculates the maximum potential revenue that each business or space could generate in a perfect world—that is, if every customer spent the most the market could bear and if traffic reached its physical limits." Then he "subtracts actual sales from that hypothetical number and calls the difference a loss, even if the venue is making money."

The remedy is extreme: Gamal blows things up and starts over again. This can be a bit of a hard sell when the enterprise is already a big moneymaker, and MGM Grand was the most profitable part of MGM Mirage Group when Gamal took charge in late 2000. But he prevailed by attacking Gatsby's, an MGM Grand restaurant with $2.1 million in sales. Gamal showed his board that Gatsby's actually was losing $3 million in potential revenue.

He brought in celebrity chef Michael Mina, renamed the place Nobhill, and the restaurant "pulled in $6.5 million in sales." Gamal performed similar magic with the Grand's hair salon. He brought in "celebrity stylist Christophe," and haircuts that used to be $55 were priced at $110 to $400, while "revenue . . . increased by 40 percent and profit by 23 percent."

The basic idea was to turn the Grand into a destination and not just somewhere to stay. "We were a dormitory," said Gamal. "People were sleeping here and going somewhere else to party."

The Grand's twenty-ninth floor, its penthouse, was also Gamalized. It was converted into "a chic hotel-within-a-hotel dubbed Skylofts, which [attracted] both convention-goers and moneyed Gen-Xers, pushing the occupancy rate up to 74 percent (from 50 percent). Revenue, meanwhile, went up 90 percent," and the Grand's Broadway-style showcase called EFX, which used to star David Cassidy or Tommy Tune, was replaced by Cirque du Soleil's *Ka*, housed in a new $160 million theater. Compared to EFX, Cirque sold six times the number of tickets.

The bottom line: "The new venues . . . boosted total sales by more than 25 percent since 2003, making the Grand only one of two casinos (along with the Bellagio) to surpass $1 billion in revenue while the annual operating profit . . . zoomed up by 45 percent."

- **Extreme profitability can require extreme measures, but it is always about what's most relevant to customers.**

Costco Profits

When Wall Street complained that Costco didn't put shareholders first, CEO Jim Sinegal said he had a different order of priorities, as reported by Kris Hudson in the *Wall Street Journal*.

"We want to obey the law, take care of our customers, take care of our people, and respect our suppliers," said Jim. "And we think if we do those four things pretty much in that order, we're going to reward shareholders." He added, "By the way, we sell for a pretty rich multiple." Costco's 514 club stores were expected to top $65 billion in 2007, and at the time Costco was trading at 21.2 times its projected per-share earnings.

Jim also had a ready response to those who said that giving customers a great bargain cost Costco profits: "There are all sorts of opportunities where you can try to sneak in a little more margin here and a little more profitability there, but that's not what we're about," he explained. "When you start suggesting that it's not important to save the customer money on this because they'll never know the difference, you start to fool yourself. The customer trusts us. You don't want to give up on that type of reputation."

Jim's favorite example is the time Costco bought up "several million pairs of Calvin Klein jeans." As Jim recalled, "Every department store was selling them for $50. We could easily have said, 'Well, we're selling every pair that we get. . . . Why not sell these for $29.99?' But we didn't. We sold them for $22.99 because we made such a great buy."

The other Costco knock is that it pays its people too much money. Said Jim, "We think that you get what you pay for. If you hire good people, pay them good wages, and provide good jobs and careers, good things will happen in your business. . . . We are the low-cost provider of merchandise, and yet we pay the highest wages. Wouldn't that suggest we're getting better productivity?"

- **Greater margins do not necessarily result in greater profits. Relevant pricing can more than make up the difference.**

Rawlings Primo

There are cases, of course, in which spending more does not necessarily lead directly to making more. As reported by Matthew Boyle in *Fortune*, Rawlings spent two years coming up with the $400 Primo baseball glove, using "Italian leather hand-sewn into an advanced three-layer design that Rawlings claimed could be broken in to suit specific positions."

The glove's design was inspired by double-walled bats, which "have a barrel made of two layers . . . which can flex more than a single layer and create a sort of trampoline effect." Similarly, the Primo featured an extra layer designed to accelerate the break-in process. "To stay on top, we continually have to come up with better gloves," said Ted Sizemore, who was promoting the glove for Rawlings.

It sounded like a dream except for one thing: Few players were willing to part with the gloves they already had. As Yogi Berra once put it, "There's nothing more personal than your own baseball glove." So it didn't matter that Primo might be the "world's best ball glove." Big leaguers were not about to give up "their well-worn, perfectly broken-in gloves." If nothing else, it might be bad luck, and no amount of financial incentive was likely to break that spell.

True enough, but as Matt Arndt of glove-making rival Easton Sports pointed out, "Innovating is cool as long as you keep in mind that current gloves are not broken."

- **What if you created the perfect baseball glove but nobody wanted to try it? Rawlings forgot what was relevant and went down swinging.**

Crowbar Marketing

The next time a bean counter tells you that spending extra money won't result in any extra sales, consider telling them that it's not just about sales—it's about relevance, and about growth.

Real growth requires the kind of innovation that gets customers excited, and that kind of innovation often means just putting a crowbar in it.

- **Even the staunchest budget hawk will understand when you insist that you can't cost-cut your way to growth. And if that doesn't work, tell them Ringo sent you.**

CHAPTER 7

Design

Yellow Is Number One

Yellow wakes me up in the morning. Yellow gets me
on the bike every day. Yellow has taught me the true
meaning of sacrifice. Yellow makes me suffer.
Yellow is the reason I am here.
—LANCE ARMSTRONG

Much of the world knows exactly why "yellow" is so extraordinarily relevant to Lance Armstrong: It's the color of the Tour de France winner's jersey.

Of course, yellow is also now inextricably associated with Lance's fight against cancer, thanks mostly to the millions of yellow LiveStrong bracelets designed and sold by Nike to raise money for cancer research. That so much meaning could be conveyed by one color speaks to the power of simplicity in design. It was indeed amazing how a back-bench hue like yellow could become cooler than blue even if just for a short while.

It might have been just a coincidence that yellow became a "hot" color for hot cars at the precise time LiveStrong bracelets were at their peak, but it probably wasn't. Ford was out with a "screaming yellow" Mustang, BMW was offering a "liquid yellow" Mini Cooper, and Hyundai's HCD-8 was moving the metal in "ballistic yellow." At the time, yellow actually was only the tenth most popular color for sport and compact cars, according to the Dupont Automotive Color Popularity Register. But dealers liked it because they thought it was triggering impulse sales.

As Lauren Boettcher of PPG Industries told Lisa Kalis of the *New York Times*, "Carmakers are needing to redefine their brands. . . . There's no better way to do it than with bright yellow." How much simpler could it be?

Flying Colors

Meanwhile, the notion that a yellow vehicle was a noticed vehicle was not lost on DHL, the shipping company. If you're near a window, take a look outside; odds are that you'll spot one of DHL's yellow trucks. If you don't, wait five minutes, and you'll almost certainly see one. Those trucks seem to be everywhere even though, obviously, they are not.

If you think back, you may remember that DHL's trucks used to be white with kind of a maroon logo. But you never, ever, noticed those trucks. They just blended in like white noise. Now that they've been repainted a hot yellow with an equally eye-popping red logo, DHL's trucks are harder to miss than a jug of Tide at your local bodega. That was really important for DHL because it had just entered the U.S. market in a big way after acquiring Airborne Express. Even though DHL had been the number one shipping concern outside the United States, its yellow was a distant third behind Federal Express and UPS stateside.

Almost overnight the company repainted some seventeen thousand trucks in a vibrant shade of yellow. The package-shipping company also yellowfied twenty thousand worker uniforms, 467 service centers, sixteen thousand drop boxes, and more than 275 pieces of paper—at a cost of some $40 million. The rebadging of DHL was not limited to paint jobs, of course. It was backed by a $110 million marketing campaign.

I asked Karen Jones, DHL's vice president of advertising, about the color choice and whether it was a direct response to UPS's now-famous "brown" campaign. Surprisingly, she said it wasn't. "I hate to burst anyone's bubble," she said, "but yellow and red were the colors chosen by our headquarters over in Germany. We really can't take any credit for it here in the United States." Karen did say that the colors were selected "to convey energy and entrepreneurialism . . . for the boldness and assertiveness and confident tone" of DHL. Then she added, "There's a joke internally . . . which is that 'yellow is number one and brown is number two.' But that probably doesn't bear repeating." (Sorry, Karen. I couldn't resist.)

I also asked Karen what she learned from DHL's branding experience. She mentioned several things but above all emphasized the importance of sticking with the vision and backing it with sufficient resources: "At a lot of companies, the marketing budget is the first thing that gets cut during hard times. But our leadership knows how critical marketing is to us at this point in our journey and does everything it can to protect that."

What is impressive is that, like Lance Armstrong, DHL staked its entire identity on a color. In a nation where states are classified as red or blue and where every team, school, and horse farm has its colors, it is remarkable that so few brands have color-coded their marketing strategies like DHL.

- **The right color could be all the relevance your brand needs.**

Tactile Tactics

While the power of color as an element of relevant design is beyond question, the most overlooked sense in marketing actually is the sense of touch, according to a story by Andy Johnson in *CTV News.* Not that there's anything new about it: "In fact, the iconic Coca-Cola bottle is one of the earliest examples of a product that came in a package so unique it could be identified by feel alone, even buried in a cooler full of ice and other bottled beverages," commented consultant Duncan Berry of Applied-Iconography.

More recent and less well known was the packaging for GlaxoSmithKline's Alli, the fat-blocking pill. "The drug comes with a reinvented pillbox called a 'shuttle' that carries the medication. It has a unique shape, can be opened with one hand, and is made with soft rubber and careful texturing that is pleasing to the touch."

As Duncan Berry observed, "It's almost like you're grabbing the hand of a friend, almost a clasp, that's a very subtle but direct connection to the idea of someone who's going along this journey with you—a friend and an ally."

Martin Lindstrom, author of *Brand Sense*, said such tactile opportunities are for the taking. "In fact," he said, "83 percent of all the communication you and I are exposed to every day is only appealing to the sense of sight." Martin also thinks tactile branding is the next big thing, saying, "I know from studies we conducted recently that 35 percent of the largest brands in the world—so the first one hundred brands—right now are working on a sensory branding strategy." He adds that tactile tactics work because humans are "hardwired" to judge people and things based on the way they feel, a habit that started with the handshake "as a way of assessing an enemy's strength and of ensuring they were unarmed."

Perhaps most important, the sense of touch "has the ability to transcend borders, languages, and cultures." Randall Frost, author of *The Globalization of Trade*, suggests that touch has the potential to be "the lingua franca of global branding."

■ **What could be more relevant than staying "in touch" with your customer?**

Quiet Design

If the sense of touch is underdeveloped in design, the effects of sound often are under attack. The reason is that people tend to associate quiet with quality. This is especially true in automotive design. The problem, according to a *Wall Street Journal* article by Jonathan Welsh, is that as car designs change, so do the noises they tend to make. When cars are modified for power and acceleration, their engines become noisier. Since they are designed "to steer precisely and handle well on a variety of roads, carmakers have made suspension springs, shock absorbers, and even tires firmer. As a result, these parts tend to transmit more vibrations to the interior in the form of road noise."

Larry Mihalko of General Motors said, "If you address ninety-nine out of one hundred problems, you wind up sabotaging the whole process." Maybe he shouldn't try so hard, or maybe he should think less about silence and more about parlaying the noises a car makes into part of its brand identity. After all, some people think that the greatest classical masterpiece of all time is John Cage's *4'33"*, in which a musician sits at the piano for four minutes and thirty-three seconds and does nothing much other than bow when the time is up. The performance, however, is far from silent. As Peter Gutmann wrote in the *Wall Street Journal*, "It's true that no music comes from the stage as concertgoers expect, but there's plenty of sound, albeit from unconventional sources. The audience soon becomes aware of immersion in a universe of audio sensation from the mundane to the profound—shifting in seats, air-conditioning, passing traffic, one's own heartbeat."

What's so great about that? Well, for one thing, said Peter, the "silence invites one's memories and gives rise to associations." As a result, the experience "is deeply personal, as no two people will experience it the same way." For another, said Peter, "the components of 'Four Thirty-three,' while capricious, surely qualify as music. Even abject noise entails the interrelationship of distinct tones, durations, volumes, rhythms, and timbre. And, like all art, it combines arbitrary conventions, preconceived structure, and customary materials with flexible personal input to create meaning that transcends actual content."

And perhaps most important, it makes the listener an active participant in the composition, versus a passive absorber of someone else's music. As such, Peter concluded, 4'33" remains "ever fresh. Its open design, sly humor, cosmic vision, and intimate scope ensure its timeless appeal, boundless vitality, and universal relevance."

■ **Silence may be golden, but relevant noises can make the cash register ring.**

Dream Cruisers

Many of the most interesting design stories emanate from the automotive industry. In some ways this is ironic, given the bland design values of so many cars these days. Several of the stories are really about design concepts, not cars that are actually being marketed, suggesting that much of the auto industry has a problem not only with relevance but also with reality.

It does seem that the only cars that truly "speak" to their drivers are cars that were designed a very long time ago. Driving home that point is the annual Woodward Dream Cruise, held every year on the third Saturday in August, as noted by Mark Yost in a *Wall Street Journal* essay. Mark observed that Detroit's automakers make the mistake of showing up—a mistake because seeing their "ovoid schlockmobiles of today" next to the great muscle cars of yesteryear "only reminds you of just how far the industry has fallen." Indeed, the Dream Cruise is "the world's largest rolling muscle-car show," featuring "cars with names like Chevelle, Mustang, and Hemi 'Cuda."

The thing you have to keep in mind, said Mark, "is that these weren't the specialty cars that Detroit made for car shows and drag racers. These were the cars that Detroit once mass-produced. Our dads drove them to work, and our moms took them to the grocery store." That was back in "the days when Detroit actually made cars with some sense of styling and git-up-and-go under the hood." Sadly, that git-up-and-go done git-up-and-went.

- **Great exciting design can be the difference between relevance and indifference.**

Citroën Rendezvous

Citroën's classic DS is far from an American muscle car. Heck, it's French, for crying out loud. But it stokes similar passions among its fans. In fact, the "oddballs" who love the Citroën DS get together every year in Saratoga Springs at the Citroën Rendezvous, reports Richard S. Chang in the *New York Times*.

For the past twenty-six years Robert Monteleone, who has been obsessed with Citroëns since he was fourteen years old, has been among them. Robert said that from the first moment he saw a Citroën, "he saw something of himself, which he could not yet define." Only later did he realize he was gay. Since then Robert has owned as many as three Citroëns at a time and currently owns two, including a 1967 Citroën DS 19, which he bought in 1993.

Robert's Citroën DS attraction is certainly understandable, given that "it is often cited as one of the top designs of the last century." An essay by Roland Barthes described the DS as "the beginnings of a new phenomenology of assembling, as if one progressed from a world where elements are welded to a world where they are juxtaposed and held together by sole virtue of their wondrous shape, which of course is meant to prepare one for the idea of a more benign Nature." It was also "a technological marvel for its time." The Citromatic transmission let drivers shift gears without a clutch, for example. The car also has that "hydro-pneumatic suspension" and its "headlights turned with the steering wheel." Ooh-la-la. That last feature actually got the Citroën banned from America.

In any case, the car didn't sell well in the States and was withdrawn from the U.S. market in 1974. According to Robert, it is precisely that rejection "by the American mainstream" that gives the Citroën its appeal. Robert said he and his fellow Citroën aficionados were "sort of quirky oddballs . . . just drawn to the commonality of loving the design and innovation."

- **Design can find its relevance in sometimes mysterious ways; the trick is leveraging that mystery into profitable sales.**

Vintage Volvos

Volvo's old designs are loved for one reason—they are simple to repair, reported Jim Motavalli in the *New York Times*. At least that is why General Colin L. Powell loves old Volvos. It seems that General Powell, when he was chairman of the Joint Chiefs of Staff, "was often found behind the chairman's quarters" tinkering with old Volvos. He admits: "At one time I had six, stashed at various places around the post so the MP's wouldn't find them all. . . . My usual pattern was to fix them mechanically and then do enough body work to get them through a quick Earl Scheib paint job."

General Powell's affinity for fixing Volvos isn't all that uncommon. Volvos never were as hip as, say, Volkswagens in the 1960s, but they were attractive to some people because they were considered reliable and inexpensive. But most of all they were "designed to be easy to fix," which largely explains their enduring popularity among tinkerers like Colin Powell.

Phil Singher, whose passion is a 122S sedan, explained: "I learned to work on the Volvo out of necessity, but the more I fixed it, the better I liked it." Gretchen Adams of the Volvo Club of America said, "The loyalty toward these older models is just unbelievable."

Volvo is happy to encourage the tinkering and still supports its vintage models; it is relatively easy to obtain parts through Volvo dealers. And if you can't find what you need, just ask a certain former U.S. secretary of state who is known to strip Volvos and stack their parts. "A lot of people heard I was doing that," he said. "Word got around among Volvo aficionados: 'If you want a starter, see General Powell.'"

■ **That Volvos were designed to be easy to fix is not only relevant to tinkerers but it also stokes a kind of loyalty that dies hard.**

Harley's Throwback

Harley-Davidson's problem, circa 2007, was that the average age of its customers was forty-six. Its solution was the Nightster, a stripped-down version of its entry-level Sportster that

Rich Christophe designed for people much like himself. In other words, age twenty-seven, not forty-six. At the time, Harley-Davidson was one hundred and the Sportster was fifty. Rich started by removing all the chrome and redesigning the Sportster for speed.

"I went back to the immediate post–World War II period when GIs came back and rode used Army bikes," he said. "They took off everything they could for speed—the front fender, a lot of the back fender."

Instead of "hanging a stoplight from the fender," he combined its function with the turn signal lamps, as is typical on cars. That allowed him to put the license plate off to the left. "I wanted people to wonder if it was legal," said Rich. It was legal, although it did give Harley's legal department fits—but that was exactly Rich's point.

- **By putting its license place where it is not supposed to be, Harley hoped to reignite its relevance among young bikers.**

Times Infiniti

Like Harley-Davidson, Infiniti has tried to use design to appeal to a new generation of potential customers. Like Karen Jones of DHL, Jan Thompson, a former vice president of marketing of Nissan North American (Infiniti's parent company), told me that commitment from the top is key—especially when the goal is to change perceptions.

"The hardest part probably is just communicating the new identity to consumers because for years they built an impression about you, and changing that impression takes time," Jan said. "Vehicle by vehicle, campaign by campaign, you slowly change people's opinions of a brand. Sometimes it takes decades. If you want to change, you have to be consistent or you'll lose your consumers. And you've got to be patient."

After an initial burst of success, Nissan's design-driven strategy faltered. But the company's approach offered insights into what's involved when design is placed at the center of a brand's marketing strategy. For one thing, it meant going out on a limb with designs that were not meant to appeal to everybody. According to Jan, Nissan's designs were polarizing—by design.

"That's just the outcome of design," she said. "That's the risk when you break out of the pack and say that you're not going to make an ordinary vehicle. When you're in a challenger role, as Nissan is—and certainly as we were in 1999—you've got to come out swinging, and you can't come out swinging with something that's vanilla. You need Neapolitan."

For Infiniti that approach was summed up using the term "vibrant design," which Jan said was the "soul of the Infiniti brand" and was represented "by using a single stylized brushstroke that conveyed the lightness of the vehicle as well as its spirit and style. It's a Japanese art form," she continued, "a kind of calligraphy called Shodo." She stressed that she wasn't talking only about visual design: "It's all five senses coming together to create a more holistic design positioning. I can sit here in the morning, and I can tell that an Infiniti FX35 just pulled into the parking lot.

"This total design platform is our strength and it distinguishes our brand in the luxury segment. When you can hear it and not even have to look at it to recognize it, that's pretty powerful."

■ **Design that is relevant to one driver may be just plain ugly to another. Nissan bravely took that chance.**

Feature Creep

"This phenomenon, generated by market forces, media hype, and twitchy retailers, creates a cycle in which products are constantly improved even if they don't need to be," wrote Allen Salkin in the *New York Times.* He was talking about "feature creep" or "the incessant rush of innovation that pushes manufacturers to tamper with products that consumers feel are already perfect."

The issue is particularly pronounced in the running-shoe category. "There's this need to continue to evolve and have consumers feel like things are getting better and that the needle is being moved even if it isn't," said David Willey of *Runner's World* magazine.

Feature creep is also in evidence in cosmetics: "When Lancôme discontinued a moisturizer called Nutrix in 2004 to make way for a new version, Nutrix Royal, the company received more than one thousand phone calls, email messages, and letters from bewildered devotees." Lancôme eventually relented and reintroduced the original.

MAC Cosmetics, meanwhile, created "a section on its Web site called Goodbyes, where it sells limited editions or discontinued products such as Speed Demon Lip Varnish."

In cars, BMW has evolved "from a nimble and relatively small car" of the 1980s into a "heavy luxury liner" today. A Honda spokesperson also admits that the company "might have abandoned its old customer base, those who want small, practical, inexpensive cars." It responded by introducing "the compact $13,850 Fit wagon . . . and sold all fifty thousand imported into the United States."

Some companies, however, see the value of sticking "with a successful product even as fashions change. . . . Since 1993, Casio has been selling the same dependable digital watch, model F30-9, for $7.95, with the same functions—time and date in a black case on a black band, nothing more.

And between 1983 and 2007 the company sold 45 million of its G-Shock series of digital watches. Casio planned to celebrate its twenty-fifth anniversary in 2008 with "a special version of its first model, the DW-500, which came only in black." This time it would be white. As Casio's David Johnson explained, "White is wicked hot in watches right now."

■ **Relevant brands are less interested in the whizbang of
bells and whistles than in the elegance of simple ideas
that work.**

Strange Bedfellows

Michael Gibbert of Bocconi University and David Mazursky
of Hebrew University think that too many brands make the
mistake of trying to innovate within their own categories, resulting in incremental innovation at best and feature glut at
worst, culminating in products that are actually less useful. It
is better, they said in a *Wall Street Journal* article, to look into
"cross-breeding" with "dissimilar and even highly remote product categories to spark the conception of a truly new product."

Perhaps most famously, Apple and Nike have collaborated
to create a sneaker iPod for joggers. In some cases such hybrids
may barely rise above the level of novelty, but in the Nike/iPod
example, the iPod doesn't just enable the runner to listen to
music but also "displays information about the number of miles
run, the pace, and calories burned."

Similarly, LG Electronics created a glucose phone that not
only uses the phone's technology to display results of a glucose
test but "can even automatically send the results via text message to caregivers."

The hard part, of course, is looking "beyond apparent in-
compatibilities of highly remote products to identify possible

matching points." Michael and David's advice is "to observe what other main product is involved in your product's usage or consumption and how the two can be beneficially combined." Think about how product functions could be modified when combined and how to create dependencies between those functions. The resulting innovations, they said, can "seem disarmingly obvious in retrospect and make one wonder why no one thought of them before."

■ **Fresh relevance in new-product design can be found by combining dissimilar products.**

Failure 101

That "everything that's designed fails, and everything that fails leads to better design" is a key point of a book by Henry Petroski called *Success Through Failure*, as reviewed by Edward Rothstein in the *New York Times*. For example, "Aleve won't be packed in child-proof bottles so difficult to open that they stymie the arthritic patients seeking the pills inside." But while more is learned from failure than success, the limiting factor is time. The reason there has been "a major bridge disaster every thirty years" is that the lessons learned over the course of a generation become taken for granted; premises are no longer scrutinized.

Too much focus on fixing failures can have a stultifying effect, however.

"Because of safety and liability fears, for example, new children's playgrounds never seem to have seesaws or 'monkey bars,' sacrificing some of the daring enterprise that once accompanied play's inherent risk."

A similar principle applies to two products in particular, the manual lawn mower and the iPod, which Edward Rothstein suggested pointed to the importance of success, not failure, in design. The manual mower, said Edward, is an "elegant" tool designed for a specific purpose. Its "flaws" were later fixed by "electric and gas mowers," which not only produced their own flaws but also eliminated "the quiet pleasure" of the manual mower and the "direct connection between the physical act of pushing and the physical result of cutting."

The iPod, meanwhile, has been celebrated for its design while its "flaws . . . are constantly being ameliorated, with increased storage, decreased size, and dedicated volume controls. But one reason for this evolution is not that it has flaws but that advancing technology makes more things possible. And its limitations are also its strengths: The iPod required a computer and could not play music for multiple listeners, so it drew other pieces of equipment into its orbit, turning the sound system and the computer into extensions of its power."

Edward imagined that "far less than thirty years from now" the iPod's limitations will be "fixed," but the iPod might lose some of its "power and beauty, . . . simplicity and clarity," and "sensual pleasure" in the process.

■ **Relevant brands aren't afraid to fail, but they never forget
what made them successful in the first place.**

Simple Wii

The very same thing that made game developers wary of the
Wii subsequently attracted them, reported Matt Richtel and
Eric A. Taub in the *New York Times*. That "thing" was simplicity. Developers "were initially cautious about the console because the Wii was less technologically sophisticated."
They also weren't sure consumers would "take to its un-
orthodox game play, which uses a motion-controlled wand
that players move to direct action on the screen." But those
doubts were dispelled once the Wii began outselling the Xbox
360 and PS3 and developers began to appreciate that they
could "create games in less time" because of the Wii's simpler graphics.

Kelly Flock, a former executive vice president of game developer THQ, said that "the budget for a Wii game ranged from
$1.5 million to $4 million, compared with the $10 million to
$12 million" spent on a PS3 or Xbox 360 game. He also said it
took only about a year to create a Wii game versus two to three
years for the others. "The Wii is a godsend," said Kelly, adding
that he was "aggressively looking for more Wii titles." In addition, noted Scott A. Steinberg, vice president of marketing at
game developer Sega of America, it took just "fifteen to

twenty-five programmers to develop a Wii title, compared with fifty or more for a PS3 or Xbox 360 game."

Given these differences in both time and money, "a developer would need to sell 300,000 copies of a Wii game to break even, compared with 600,000 of a game for the PS3 or Xbox 360."

- **Keeping Nintendo Wii's design simple heightened its relevance not only to consumers but also to the game designers who were so critical to its success.**

HondaJet Engines

One of his bosses called him "the stupidest engineer I've ever met in my life," but that didn't stop Michimasa Fujino from pushing through a radical design idea that promised to hand Honda a quick 10 percent of the small-jet market, reported Norihiko Shirouzu in the *Wall Street Journal*.

Michimasa's innovation, the HondaJet, put "the engines above the wings" instead of under them "or on the rear of the fuselage." Conventional wisdom said that engines above wings put a "drag on the plane," but Michimasa thought differently based on an "air-flow calculation" he discovered "in a 1930s aeronautics textbook."

Michimasa's design, as it turned out, cruised "8 percent faster" and was able to take off and land on shorter runways than "the roughly similar Cessna Citation CJ1+." It was also more fuel efficient: The $3.65 million HondaJet used "about 22 percent less fuel than the Citation, flying, for instance, at 441 miles an hour and at an altitude of 35,000 feet."

Its cabin space was "also nearly 20 percent larger," and it featured a cargo area that was 45 percent roomier than Citation's. All of that at a price that was $880,000 lower than the Cessna and had "the fit and finish of a luxury car." So what if putting the engines over the wings looked a little scary?

Michimasa prevailed by convincing Honda's top management that this jet would be the flying equivalent of the Honda Civic, tapping into their desire to be seen as innovative by creating something other than an ordinary airplane. The HondaJet is expected to be on the market by about 2010, more than twenty years after Michimasa began developing it. He commented, "A lot of companies try to cut into the small-jet business, but most of them . . . repeat the same mistakes. If Honda had done it the same way and did not learn all the skills and technologies involved from scratch, we couldn't have come up with the design we have today."

■ **Honda's simple but daring design idea resulted not only in the relevance of a faster, cheaper airplane but also in a bold new image of innovation.**

Whirlpool Metrics

Chuck Jones knew he needed a new approach when his management at Whirlpool wouldn't approve a design flourish that would add five bucks to per-unit costs, reported Bill Breen in *Fast Company*. As Whirlpool's design chief, Chuck realized his jig was up when "the company's resource-allocation team asked him to estimate the return on investment." He couldn't offer one, and he got nowhere by asking for a little faith in his design instincts.

His first step was a survey of fifteen "design-centric" companies, such as BMW, Nike, and Nokia, to see how they went about "forecasting return on design. . . . To his surprise, few had a system. . . . Most simply based future investments on past performance." So Chuck and his team developed a process where customer focus groups were exposed to prototypes, and they measured their responses to issues such as aesthetics, craftsmanship, technical performance, ergonomics, and usability.

Chuck then charted "the results against both competing products and [Whirlpool's] own previous iterations, giving it a baseline of objective evidence from which to make investment decisions." It sounds a little geeky, but after two years, the approach seemed to be working for Whirlpool. For example, Whirlpool's KitchenAid Architect Series II freestanding range won top scores from the focus groups. As a result the resource-allocation folks approved "a 15 percent increase in investment over its predecessor" model, and three months after its launch "profits for the redesigned range were up 30 percent over the previous model."

Chuck became convinced his system had changed the culture at Whirlpool, enabling his design group "to make the business case for investments and give the financial folks greater confidence to ante up—resulting in bolder designs." As Chuck put it, "We can no longer get on being the wacky creatives who can't be held to any kind of standard."

- **By figuring out how to quantify the relevance of its designs, Whirlpool's designers won over the bean counters.**

Paul B. MacCready

Then there are those who refuse to be held to any kind of standard, and design amazing things as a result. Those people would include the late Paul B. MacCready.

"He believed that daydreaming was his most productive activity," Douglas Martin wrote in a *New York Times* obituary when MacCready died in September 2007. He was "an awesomely accomplished inventor who studied circling hawks and vultures to figure out how to realize the loftiest dreams of Leonardo da Vinci." His "fascination with aerodynamics came from watching butterflies and moths as a boy, and his dreams for the future included animal-powered flight." He once said, "You can do all kinds of things if you just plunge ahead. . . . It doesn't mean you're any good at them, but you can be good enough."

He also said, "I'm more interested in a world that works than what sells. . . . We make strange devices that do more with less." Among those devices was his "Gossamer Condor," the first aircraft to achieve "sustained flight by human power." It crossed the English Channel. Then came the the "Gossamer Penguin," which "made the first solar-powered climbing flight in 1980."

Seven years later Paul MacCready "and his team of young engineering zealots also invented a solar-powered car called the Sunraycer, which won a 1,867-mile race across Australia against twenty-two other solar-powered cars." His other "creations included tiny robotic planes used for military reconnaissance . . . and an eighteen-foot eerily realistic flying dinosaur for an IMAX movie." Despite such inventions, he "considered technology a mixed blessing" and once described himself as "an ambivalent Luddite."

But he wasn't at all ambivalent about innovation: "There is a value to some way-out impractical projects that are done for prizes, symbolism, or the fun of it, where you don't worry about production," he told the *New York Times* in 1990. "You can focus on extremes; when you do that, you're able to go way beyond prescribed limits to new frontiers."

■ **Relevant design can be found at the extremes, invisible to those who think *only* about what will sell.**

CHAPTER 8

Experience

What Would Warhol Do?

The people who have the best fame are those who have
their names on stores. The people with very big stores
named after them are the ones I'm really jealous of.
—ANDY WARHOL

The store Andy Warhol said he was most jealous of was
Marshall Field. But he might have felt at least a little bit
honored if he knew that twenty years after his death
the Warhol experience was alive and well at Barneys, Macy's,
Nordstrom's, and Urban Outfitters.

Most of all, Andy's spirit made the cash register ring at Barneys, whose creative director, Simon Doonan, referred to the
late pop artist as "the patron saint of retail" in a *New York
Times* article by Ruth La Ferla. Barneys featured *Warholiana*
everywhere from its holiday catalog to its shopping bags
and, of course, on merchandise—up to and including "limited-
edition Campbell's soup cans with reproductions of Warhol
labels."

Terry Teachout, writing in the *Wall Street Journal*, said that the mistake many people made about Andy Warhol was thinking he was an artist. "He was, instead, a preternaturally shrewd operator who transformed Marcel Duchamp's anti-art into glossy gewgaws suitable for mail-order merchandising," Terry wrote. "He silk-screened money."

Terry wasn't kidding. Revenues from some forty Andy Warhol licenses quadrupled over a five-year period ending in 2006, generating more than $2 million in royalties in 2006 alone. Retail sales of Warhol's licensed merchandise that year were somewhere between $40 million and $50 million in the United States, according to Michael Stone of the Beanstalk Group.

- **As Andy Warhol himself once said, "Being good in business is the most fascinating kind of art."**

Moment of Truth

Look no further than Procter & Gamble, arguably the most admired and successful marketer in U.S. history, for evidence of the importance of the shopping experience to business growth. Procter & Gamble totally galvanized itself around the concept of "the first and second moments of truth," which was first introduced by P&G's CEO A. G. Lafley about seven years ago.

Simply put, the "first moment of truth" is when a shopper

chooses a P&G brand in the store, while the "second moment of truth" occurs when the consumer experiences the product at home. Dina Howell gained great acclaim for being in charge of the "first moment of truth" for Procter & Gamble. That is a really high-profile job. As my friend Jeff McElnea joked, "You never hear about the person at P&G who is in charge of the *second* moment of truth!"

Dina told me that the "first moment of truth" is all about making and marketing brands "in a way that shoppers get what they want when they want it, and they get the kind of information they need." And she said the approach was extremely effective. "I've seen the difference it makes to shoppers when they get the right product at the right time and how much we can delight them," said Dina. "And it is making a significant difference in our business results."

■ **Being good in business is all about the experience—most of all the *shopping* experience.**

Retail as Media

"Creating an experience" is probably the most popular cliché in marketing today (if you don't count "being relevant" :-). "Experiential marketing," as some call it, can refer to anything that touches the consumer by way of the five senses. That is often just another way of saying that old-fashioned advertising—television, radio, print—simply doesn't cut it any-more. Since we have already done our hatchet job on tradi-tional advertising, we won't go back to that. Instead, let's talk about the one kind of experience that eclipses all others in terms of its potential for relevance and therefore growth for a brand. That experience is the *shopping* experience. The reasons for that are simple.

First of all, while only a portion of the population may watch any given television show, listen to any given radio program, or read any given magazine, *everybody goes shopping*. Granted, we may not all shop at the same stores, but one way or another we are far more likely to encounter your brands at a store than anywhere else. Even more important, the store is where people make purchases. If you can make the leap that the retail store is a medium for marketing (it's hardly a stretch, given that it can communicate in real time, in all dimensions, and to each of the five senses), it is arguably the only medium where mar-keting and sales can happen simultaneously.

You might make the case that sales and marketing also hap-pen on the Internet, but I would argue that very little market-ing really happens on the Internet—at least so far. The Internet is mostly a transactional medium, not a marketing medium. It certainly does not yet have the ability to surround the con-sumer in an experience as much as a retail store.

Because retail has so much potential, it is thoroughly per-plexing that so many marketers continue to regard retail as merely a distribution channel. They persist in spending untold dollars creating a wonderful image and message for their brands, while ignoring the most critical moment. Dina Howell's "first moment of truth" is when we are deciding whether to buy their brand or someone else's.

That would be the moment at the retail store. Then marketers wonder why they are not getting a satisfactory return on their marketing investments. Well, it's because nobody is thinking about their ads when they are shopping. At that point their ads are irrelevant.

Shopping for Shoppers

The imperative to understand consumers while they are in the store shopping has given rise to a relatively new discipline known as "shopper marketing."

Chris Hoyt, a widely respected consultant to consumer packaged-goods companies, said that shopper marketing is based on the premise that the minute consumers get into their cars to go shopping, they morph into a mindset that traditional demographic analysis does not anticipate or encompass. This mindset, said Chris, is driven by various "need states," such as "care for family" or "immediate consumption," which dictate what shoppers intend to buy, where they intend to buy it, and why.

According to Chris, different channels and different formats are intrinsically better suited to satisfy certain "need states" than others. For example, a shopper might pick a club store to "care for family" versus a convenience store for "immediate consumption." By understanding which need states a particular format is best suited to satisfy, retailers can ensure that each shopping trip is the best (the most *relevant*) their shoppers could experience. The result is an increase in the number of trips, higher transaction sizes, and genuine loyalty.

- **Given that retail is where sales happen, marketers should spend at least as much time thinking about what's relevant to *shoppers* as they do thinking about what's relevant to *consumers*.**

Wayfinding Loyalty

Stuart Armstrong thinks that most retailers and brand marketers have missed the opportunity to solve one of the greatest problems shoppers have. "That problem, quite simply," said Stu, "is finding their way around the damn store." That is not a problem in smaller format stores, said Stu, but it is in big-box retailers like Home Depot, Costco, and Wal-Mart. It also sometimes even afflicts midsized stores such as Barnes & Noble and CVS.

"I don't know how many books the average Barnes & Noble stocks, but I do know that I sometimes find myself frustrated because I can't find what I'm looking for," he said. Stu is president of a company called EnQii Americas, which specializes in in-store media, so he has thought a lot about the problem. His solution, as published in *The Hub* magazine, is to take "a page from commercial office buildings and create a system of touch-screen 'wayfinding' stations" that help shoppers navigate their way through the store. Stu thinks it would be even better if these stations were linked to the store's loyalty card program.

"That way," said Stu, "shoppers have the option of swiping their loyalty cards at the station and gaining the additional benefit of targeted offers or relevant information." He concluded: "What better way to improve the shopping experience than by helping shoppers find what they're looking for, when and where they're looking for it, and letting them know what else is on special that might be of interest?"

- **Relevant brands view in-store media not as just another channel for more ads but as a way to help shoppers get the most out of their shopping trips.**

Apple, Apple, Apple

Plenty of retailers—Fresh & Easy Neighborhood Market, Cabela's, Costco, and Trader Joe's, to name a few—understand the potential of retail to satisfy shopper "need states" and consider that insight a key element of their overall marketing strategy. Very few brands do. One shining exception would be Apple, of course.

What's that? Yet another story about Apple's retail strategy? It's too darn good to resist. This one comes by way of Steve Lohr, writing in the *New York Times* in May 2006, shortly after Apple opened its flagship store on Fifth Avenue in Manhattan. The story centered on Ron Johnson, the former Target Stores merchandising savant that Steve Jobs hired away to dream up and make real the stores that are now driving much of Apple's success: "Revenue for each square foot at Apple stores [in 2005] was $2,489, compared to $971 at Best Buy," according to Forrester Research.

"Sales at the stores more than doubled [in 2005], to nearly $2.4 billion, and same-store sales, those open at least a year, increased 45 percent." Yes, same-store sales did fall 18 percent in April 2006, but that drop was attributed to Apple's switch to Intel microprocessors, causing a good number of consumers to hold tight until new models were available.

Five years earlier the idea of Apple stores didn't look so promising. As Ron Johnson recounted it, Steve Jobs showed him to a conference table with four computers on it and said, "Here's our products." Ron said, "How big is the brand?" Steve said, "Apple is one of the biggest brands in the world."

So Ron set out to "design a retail experience that's as big as the space." But here was the key: "Steve felt with every bone in his body that Apple had to do retailing. . . . It was not an experiment for him. He saw it as an essential business strategy."

Compounding the risk was Steve's belief that the stores had to be in "more expensive sites, like malls and downtown areas." Ron said, "Steve's view was they'll never drive ten miles to look at us, but they will walk ten feet."

Apple Happiness

So what is it really like to shop at one of Apple's stores? As it turns out, "cool news" sometimes happens in real life, as it did when I visited an Apple store at a mall in White Plains, New York.

My old laptop was sluggish, one of our computers at the office had died, and I was champing at the bit to replace it with one of those new MacBooks—that incredibly cool-looking black one. So I started tapping away at one of the five or so flat-black MacBooks they had laid out on tables, mainly testing its speed. As a reliably geeky-looking clerk approached, I looked up and said, "I'll take one."

Well, not so fast. She started peppering me with all kinds of questions about how I planned to use the computer, what kind of software I was using, and why I wanted this particular computer. By the time she was done with her questions, I realized that this really wasn't the right computer and that I could solve my problem in a way that didn't involve buying anything at all at that Apple store that day.

I looked at her and said, "You know, you just talked me out

of buying this computer." She smiled and said, "That's okay. We just want you to be happy."

People tend to forget that when Apple first announced it was opening stores, the prevailing opinion among analysts was that Apple was about to be cored. These days most analysts fall all over themselves to praise the wisdom of Apple's retail strategy, which was developed largely because Steve Jobs wasn't happy about the way other retailers were merchandising Apple's products.

■ **Never underestimate the relevance of really smart retail.**

Fresh as Tesco

Few recent developments in the U.S. food business created as much of a stir as the news that Tesco, the United Kingdom's top retailer, planned to open about one hundred small-format stores in the American West. Leading that initiative was Simon Uwins, a twenty-three-year veteran of the Tesco organization. Simon arrived in El Segundo, California, without a format or plan—just a simple brief to find out whether there was an opportunity for Tesco.

After three years of studying the marketplace, Simon told me that Tesco decided there was. "We think we came up with a way of entering the market, which is by doing something different rather than just doing what everybody else does. We decided to do Fresh & Easy Neighborhood Market," he said.

What would make Fresh & Easy different? "When we talked to people and went into their households, we heard a fairly consistent message," said Simon. "That message was that what people wanted was fresh, affordable food—wholesome food— but they wanted it close to home. We reckon we figured out a way to deliver that to them."

Simon went on to say that Fresh & Easy would deliver that kind of experience "by keeping things simple." He said that when he talked to shoppers, they frequently complained about two things in particular: "We heard an awful lot of people first bemoaning that they had to go to lots of different stores to get what they needed and then questioning why there are so many similar products on the shelf." The solution, Simon said, was to be an "editor" for Fresh & Easy's shoppers. The goal, he said, was "to make sure you can satisfy all your regular household needs—including your favorite brands—by editing out the proliferation of similar products and also a lot of the different size variations."

As Simon put it, "Simplicity is something that seems to me is an increasing theme around the world and certainly a theme in this country. Being simple is part of what we do, and there is nothing simpler than just going and talking to people and finding out what they want and then delivering it better than anybody else."

■ **Tesco's Fresh & Easy Neighborhood Market keeps it relevant by keeping it simple.**

In the 'Hood

In addition to keeping it simple, Simon Uwins also kept it "real." In his case, that meant living up to Fresh & Easy's billing as a "neighborhood market." What exactly does it mean to be a "neighborhood market"? Here's what Simon told me about that:

> On one level, it simply means being close to people's homes. But it's also a bit more than that. It also means being a place where people are recognized. It's a friendly place. You see people from your local neighborhood and feel comfortable there.
>
> Hopefully, we'll be recruiting people to work at the stores from around the local neighborhood. It really is a store for the neighborhood and run by the neighborhood.
>
> The other side of it is that when you operate in neighborhoods, people actually expect you to be a good neighbor! For example, we won't schedule deliveries overnight to ensure that noise won't disrupt their sleep. We'll also be careful about how we route the trucks in so they don't go past schools at busy times and such like. So we'll be part of the neighborhood and considerate of the neighborhood.

■ **Being relevant carries responsibilities that begin at a neighborhood level.**

Yorkville Copy Service

Over a period of thirty-five years Bill Torres whipped up intense customer loyalty and beat back Kinko's simply by treating his customers the same way he treated his friends, reported John Eligon in the *New York Times*. In fact, his customers insisted they were his friends. "He's the quintessential mom-and-pop shop," said Kathy Jolowiz, a local historian. "In the '30s and '40s, shop owners were neighbors. Everybody knew everybody. That's gone now." Except at Yorkville Copy Service at 84th Street and Lexington Avenue in New York City, where Bill Torres and his wife, Liz, do everything except run their shop the way the chain stores do.

Yorkville Copy is "small, cluttered, and dim," and Bill's "hands are usually smeared with dry ink. . . . Part of the shop's appeal is the vintage devices that are interspersed with the modern copiers and printers. There is a century-old paper cutter, an age-old tape dispenser, and a tube radio from the 1950s that collects dust in the corner of the shop."

Bill said "that five to ten customers each week are there because a nearby chain store cannot fulfill their requests." Bill suggested that there was nothing to it. "I just give people what they want . . . going the extra yard and doing it for them, taking jobs that basically nobody else wants." He added that it is "friendliness that brings them back."

Bill started out as a Yorkville employee, buying out the store from its owners who had told him that "talking to customers . . . was a waste of time." Apparently not. When Bill turned sixty, he celebrated at a party that was fully initiated by his customers— uh—friends. It was perhaps a celebration of a time "when stores were more than just a place to make purchases."

■ **Relevance is sometimes just a matter of friendliness.**

Kiehl's Apothecary

Described as "a cross between the Smithsonian and Duane Reade," Kiehl's, the apothecary located at 109 Third Avenue in New York City since its founding in 1851, is a rare place where men and women in white coats actually put their patrons at ease, reported Mike Albo in the *New York Times.*

Kiehl's "displays druggist relics—old anatomical charts, bottles of potassium chlorate, and Epsom salt tins—in its store as if they were dioramas in the Smithsonian, which, it turns out, holds many old Kiehl's formulas in its pharmacological products collection."

The store's clerks are like relics, too—both because they dress in white lab coats and because they also take a relaxed, low-key approach to helping their customers. At Kiehl's the tone is different because it carries "no trace of sales desperation." Sure, the lady in the white coat might tell you about the many great products that may solve your health or beauty problem, but instead of pressure she gives you little samples—throws them in a bag so you can try some before you buy some.

That approach apparently dates back only to 1988 when Jami Morse, granddaughter of Irving Morse (who bought Kiehl's in 1921), took over the store. "A clever marketer, she eschewed pushy advertising and relied on word of mouth while supplying magazine editors with products and expensive gifts." Most important, "the promotional budget was put back into development of new products," most of which "are still made at its Piscataway, New Jersey, factory and delivered like fresh-baked bread every day." The kicker is that Kiehl's has been owned by L'Oréal since 2000 and "has exploded onto an international level with more than twenty-five stores worldwide."

But L'Oréal "has pledged to maintain the idiosyncratic environment and to stay as faithful as possible to the formulas Kiehl's developed over its long history." In any case, it is funny, as Mike Albo pointed out, "that the one place that actually may have sold snake oil at some time is where you feel no pressure to buy."

■ **Shoppers suffer from enough stress without being pressured at retail. Relevant retailers sell more by pushing less.**

Holding the Bag

Where is the greatest room for improvement in the shopping experience? I put that question to executives at Unilever N.A., Virgin Entertainment Group, Miller Brewing Company, Wild Oats, and CoActive Marketing Group.

Lisa Klauser, Unilever

For the packaged goods industry, it is around merchandising. We are talking a lot about shopping experiences, but when you go into a store, you still see cut-case pallets and corrugated displays. We have the opportunity to really up the game in the world of merchandising and create better experiences for consumers and shoppers while they're in the store.

Dee Mc Laughlin, Virgin

The shopping experience should be fun and discovery driven. It is not good enough anymore to have a satisfied customer because satisfied customers can switch for no reason other than just to try something else. We launched a loyalty program called VIP—Virgin Important Person. Not only do our customers earn points with every purchase, but they actually get cash back. They win instant prizes right at the register, and they are entered to win a huge sweepstakes each month. We take VIP members to meet their idols—Jay-Z, Paul McCartney, Pamela Anderson, the list goes on. Our slogan is "It's not the size of your VIP-ness . . . it's how you use it." When we sent out our first e-mail to people who had signed up for it, we had 92 percent of them come back into the store and buy something.

Ed Gawronski, Miller

What we see is more movement toward leveraging the sensory experience. We have done that with one of our brands, Leinenkugel's Sunset Wheat, where you get the experience of the orange with the beer. That's a way to bring to life different aspects of the brand, to use and leverage the sensory experience. That creates a point of difference. When consumers want something different, you have to be much more innovative and creative in how you show, present, and display the beer.

Laura Coblentz, Wild Oats

One of the biggest areas for improvement is just the experience itself. In Europe you see grocery stores that look like high-end fashion boutiques. Graphically, we put a lot of things in place in terms of imagery and colors that are more supportive and conducive of the lifestyle that Wild Oats represents versus linear, vertical rows of aisles. We want to make sure that Wild Oats doesn't look so much like a conventional grocery store as we have in the past.

Charlie Tarzian, CoActive

We've only begun to scratch the surface of a much better use of data to drive insight and to become more one to one with the retail experience. For me the high mark is the Tesco loyalty program in the United Kingdom, where they can deploy insight into their environment on a weekly basis. As a result, they can talk to people in a mass customized way.

All Small & Mighty

"Granted, it's a little hard to see how brands, whose identities are confined to boxes, cans and bags, can have a meaningful effect on the shopping experience," wrote Al Wittemen, a managing director at Tracy Locke, in *The Hub* magazine.

"However," he continued, "creating relevant solutions to their immediate needs . . . can be as simple as changing a product's formula and packaging. One packaged goods brand, All Small & Mighty detergent, is a perfect example of how an innovative approach to product packaging can improve the shopping experience. If you're not familiar with it, All Small & Mighty is a concentrated laundry detergent that comes in a much smaller package than conventional detergents."

Al went on to explain that shoppers appreciate the smaller package because it's not as heavy, requires less storage, and you don't have to buy it as often. It's also more environmentally friendly. But the most important thing about Small & Mighty, said Al, "is that it aligns with the way people shop the store." As he pointed out, most people shop the store's perimeter first before venturing down the aisles.

"What this means is, you get to the detergent aisle after you've bought your eggs, your produce, and your freshly baked goods. You pick up this big jug of laundry detergent, and you have to stop and figure out how to get it into the cart without crushing the bananas and the muffins. That may sound like a small matter, but it's not to anyone who likes their bananas without bruises!"

- **Relevant brands design their packages for relevance to shoppers at retail.**

Saved by Starbucks

Michael Gates Gill, author of *How Starbucks Saved My Life*, said he's learned that cleaning the toilets at Starbucks is more satisfying than doing advertising for Ford Motor Company, reported Joyce Wadler in the *New York Times*.

Years ago when Michael was working on the Ford account as a J. Walter Thompson advertising executive, he says he was ordered to fly out to Detroit to discuss a campaign. It was Christmas day, and his kids hadn't even finished opening their presents yet. Michael says he complied. His reward for his years of that kind of dedication was to be fired from his $160,000-a-year job at age fifty-three, he said, because the agency could replace him with "a younger person for a quarter of his salary."

JWT denies Michael's version of events, but whatever happened, it led him to a job earning $10.50 an hour at a Starbucks in Bronxville, New York. That unusual career move occurred some ten years after he started a business that ultimately failed, and about a week after he was diagnosed with a brain tumor. Michael was sitting in the Starbucks, unemployed and with no health insurance, dressed in an expensive suit and doing his best to look important. Oddly, the manager asked him if he wanted a job. The offer included health insurance, so he took it, and, Michael said, he entered a world "where everything, even cleaning grubby tiles, was given a positive spin."

It sounds just like advertising except for one thing: It was a world where everyone was treated with "respect—even homeless people who needed to use the bathroom." Indeed, while cleaning the toilet, Michael said he was "surprised by how little revulsion I felt for a job I would have previously thought beneath me."

He found comfort working "where people could be nicer and the work environment better than I had ever believed possible. . . . What you are trying to do is help other people enjoy something," he said. That "something," he explained, is not a "multimillion-dollar ad campaign. It's just trying to serve a good cup of coffee."

■ **Respect is always relevant, but most especially at retail.**

Fifteen Minutes of Retail

If Andy Warhol were alive today, he might say, "In the future, everyone will be a retailer for fifteen minutes." Actually, he would probably be so sick of that quote that he'd come up with something more interesting to say—but he'd certainly be intrigued by the concept of pop-up shops.

Pop-up shops are nothing new, having made a splash as early as 2003 when Target, among others, began toying with the idea. As the name suggests, pop-up shops are shops that pop up for a few weeks or even a few days. Usually they move into a storefront that is between tenants.

In a way, pop-up shops are the retail equivalent of a thirty-second television commercial. Song Airlines, for example, used pop-up shops to convey a sense of what it was like to fly its airline. "Shoppers" could plop down in one of Song's airline seats and sample its in-flight food as giant plasma screens projected images of sky and clouds streaming by. Unlike television commercials, however, Song's stores also rang up sales. "We took a lot of reservations out of our store in SoHo," Song's Tim Mapes told me. "The same thing happened in Boston. The stores lead to sales, to enrollments in our Sky Miles program, and they drive awareness."

J. C. Penney's Michael Cape was similarly enthusiastic about the return on investment of its pop-up shop. "It costs a minimum in the scope of the entire marketing campaign," he told *USA Today.* "What we got back outweighs the cost."

For about the cost of a television commercial, Procter & Gamble set up a pop-up shop in downtown Toronto, according to Hollie Shaw in the *Financial Post*. The shop, called Look-Fab Studio, was intended to get women to think a bit differently about P&G's health and beauty line: Cover Girl, Pantene, and Nice'n Easy. "It is the comprehensive solution sale," said Ken Wong, a marketing professor at Queen's University School of Business. "And if they can get the consumer thinking about this as a suite of products, it could be very lucrative for them."

Look-Fab Studio is described as "a brightly lit, modern showroom divided into three makeover stations. . . . Consumers are treated to mini-makeovers from Cover Girl and skin analysis from Olay, and can book a free hair color and style session courtesy of Nice'n Easy and Pantene. Smock-wearing beauty experts are on hand to give advice and detailed information about the lineup of P&G products. At the end of the hour, consumers walk out with a bag of freebies."

P&G spokesperson Joyce Law commented, "We are going out on a limb with this concept, but within P&G the philosophy is to connect with the consumer when or where she is most receptive."

Dave Lackie, editor of *Cosmetics* magazine, thought it was all very ingenious. "What I think is so clever about it is that it has really taken the VIP experience of a swag suite (which doles out gift bags to celebrities at promotional parties and entertainment-industry festivals) and given the average consumer access to that." He added, "Having these space-age makeover pods for each of these different brands elevates them all into the realm of higher-end beauty. They are taking mass products and giving them more equity. Crest toothpaste becomes oral fashion. And judging from the mobs that are in that store, they are totally buying into it."

Whether pop-up shops endure beyond their own fifteen minutes of fame remains to be seen. What will endure is the indisputable truth that retail is not only bursting with creative marketing potential but also inherently accountable for sales results. What could be more critical to consider when "accountability" weighs so heavily on the future of marketing? Indeed, with the gulf between marketing and sales—between a brand and its return on marketing investment—as wide as ever, it is worth asking one very simple question: What would Warhol do?

■ **Relevant brands have figured out that retail is not just a distribution channel; it is where experiences are created and sales are made.**

CHAPTER 9

Value

The Value of Value

All the advertising in the world doesn't really help if
you're not adding any value to the brand.
—SCOTT DEAVER

ll the advertising in the world meant less than nothing on September 11, 2001. It is uncomfortable to
write those words even several years later because
doing so trivializes what happened on that day. Of course, almost everything seems trivial by comparison. It always will.
With that in mind, let's talk about how one advertiser, Avis,
responded to the situation. As Scott Deaver, Avis's executive
vice president of strategy, told me, the company's president,
Bob Salerno, and the people who were working with him at the
time simply told local managers to help people get home.

"The directive," said Scott, "was to take care of people first
and to worry about the cars later." He continued, "It cost the
company a lot of money. It caused the company a lot of

problems, too, because so much of our fleet was then out of place. But the Avis culture is designed for this kind of empowerment. It was a great moment for Avis."

Indeed it was, although what Avis did that day was neither little noted nor long remembered. That hardly mattered because the Avis response was not a one-off fluke; as Scott Deaver noted, it was consistent with the brand's culture—its values and the way it views its relationships with its customers. Avis doesn't just deliver value to its customers. It makes its customers *feel valued*, too. As my friend Todd Waters likes to point out, most brands knock themselves out trying to make consumers loyal to their brands. What they usually forget is that it is even more important to make sure their brands are loyal to their customers.

There is little chance that an advertising slogan will drive on either side of that two-way street. Ironically, however, Avis's culture is, in fact, rooted in its advertising slogan, "We Try Harder," which is now more than forty years old. Today, for Avis, the slogan is much more than a clever headline, said Scott: "Originally, it simply meant that we're number two, so we try harder. Now it means we try harder because we have to have a better product to justify a premium price. It is right for our brand space because Avis is supposed to go the extra mile, do extra things, and love our customers more. It is symbolically great but also great from a practical business standpoint. We're going after a big market with product innovation."

In other words, it is more than forty years later, and Avis is finding a whole new set of ways to stick it to Hertz. In many ways this transition from ad slogans to customer services is a metaphor for what has happened to the business of marketing over the years. Even though Hertz is still number one in airport car rentals and spends something like five times as much on advertising, Avis has repeatedly beaten Hertz in surveys rating customer loyalty to brands. When I asked Scott Deaver why, here's what he said:

> *Well, a couple of things work in our favor. One is that Avis is more focused on excellence in customer service than any company I've ever worked for. And I mean focused. Everybody thinks about customer service all the time. Everybody is measured for it. People are dead serious about fixing the things that are wrong and making the good things even better. That focus really does pay off in a better customer experience.*
>
> *The second thing is, if you dig into research about Avis and Hertz, what you find is that Hertz tends to get credit for high-tech products and innovation. Avis tends to get credit for "people" values. One of the things that enables us to at least go toe-to-toe with Hertz is that we're focused on those values. We're true to them. We build in that brand space. We have that real, unique, and differentiated position in the car rental market that gives us a lot of strength.*

The obvious question, then, is why is Avis still number two? Here is what Scott had to say about that:

There are several reasons. Hertz's corporate strategy is built around "number oneness." They have a couple of big key accounts and make financial sacrifices to hold on to them for volume's sake. At this company, the focus is on profitability and service excellence, and not just volume.

That leads us to decisions that are not driven by what's going to make us the biggest. It's driven by what's going to make us most profitable for our shareholders and the best company for our customers. We don't have any particular commitment to being bigger than Hertz.

- **Avis may be "number two," but its relevance is all about making its customers "number one."**

Rental Gymnastics

While Scott Deaver certainly emphasizes the value of values, much of the car rental industry—as well as many other product and service categories—seems to focus more on their prices. In fact, some car rental companies change prices as many as "ten, twenty, or more times a day," causing prices to "rise 50 percent or more, or drop at least 20 percent within twenty-four hours," reported Gary Stoller in *USA Today*.

"It is confusing out there for customers," said Mike Kane, a car rental consultant, who observed that most consumers aren't aware of the price fluctuations. Sue Reiss is one such consumer, and she said she is pretty shocked. "If the cars are available, why would there be a reason to vary those prices?" she asked.

Richard Broome of Hertz said the price changes usually occur "when unexpected severe weather shuts down an airport, and we have a run on cars rented one-way, leaving us with no cars for the next day." Some say, however, that the changes are necessary because consumers now use the Internet to monitor prices, forcing the car rental companies to change prices more frequently to stay competitive.

"A small price drop can result in more bookings, and a minor increase can bring in a lot of revenue," according to Mike Kane. Prices change most frequently for cars that are in highest demand—that is, "compact, intermediate, and full-size cars." They also change more frequently at bigger airports versus smaller ones, and change less frequently at nonairport rental sites where rental fees are usually lower to begin with.

The car rental companies say the best advice is simply to book as far in advance as possible because prices go up the closer you book to your arrival date. Frank Stasiowski, a frequent renter, said the variable pricing stinks but that he copes by questioning his rate at pickup time. "About fifty percent of the time the manager lowers my rate magically," he said.

■ **Relevant pricing is not only what looks appealing on your spreadsheet but what makes sense to your customers.**

Driving Value

Perceptions of value seem to explain why two cars—Pontiac Solstice and Saturn Sky—are not equally successful even though they are essentially the same car. In fact, Saturn's Sky is outselling Pontiac's Solstice even though Solstice features a lower price.

That wasn't always true, though. According to a *New York Times* article by Nick Bunkley, when Solstice was first introduced, it created so much head-turning excitement that consumers "paid as much as $6,000 above the sticker price to be among the first in their neighborhood to have one." By late 2007, dealers were reporting an oversupply of the Solstice, with some "trying to push them out the door by cutting as much as $1,000 off the sticker price." Saturn's Sky, meanwhile, continued to enjoy strong demand, to the point where some buyers reportedly had to "wait several weeks or months for their Sky to arrive."

So what went wrong for Solstice? "Saturn, although it had been struggling, had nowhere near the type of negative baggage that the Pontiac brand did," said Wes Brown, an automotive consultant. He added, "That brand is damaged. If you ask the average person, I don't think he could tell you what the brand's supposed to be." In other words, as cool as the Solstice looked, ultimately its image was such a big disconnect from Pontiac's image that consumers couldn't reconcile it. The Solstice example "is evidence not only of how quickly the luster on stylish cars can fade but also how difficult it is for an automotive brand to win back customers once they have been put off."

When Fiat reintroduced its classic entry-level 500 model, it hoped to follow in the footsteps of the BMW Mini and return Fiat to profitability. Its success, according to a *Wall Street Journal* article by Kenneth Maxwell, hinged on the balance of price and value.

"The crux of the discussion on the 500 is price," said analyst Stephen Cheetham. "Will consumers think it is special enough to pay a premium versus all the other perfectly competent entry-level cars on the market?"

The 500—a three-door—started at about $16,000, "with a range of engines and the latest in in-car gadgetry offered as extras." The trouble was that, unlike BMW, Fiat was not exactly known for its quality, which meant prospective owners were going to be especially sensitive to value.

"People don't buy the BMW Mini just because of nostalgia for the old Mini," said Stuart Whitwell, a brand valuation consultant. "They are also buying a BMW because they're getting a quality car." He also questioned whether the Fiat 500 was "iconic enough" outside Italy. Others noted that the VW Beetle ultimately faltered because of its relatively high price.

■ **You are what you charge—and such perceptions rarely change.**

Tata Motors

While Fiat took aim at maximizing its price, India's Tata Motors was heading in the opposite direction. Tata's goal, according to a *Forbes* article by Robyn Meredith, was to offer a car costing just $2,500, making it "the cheapest, by far, ever made."

Ratan Tata, the company's chairman, fully accepted the nature of providing that much value at so little cost. "They are still saying it can't be done," he admitted. Part of the plan was to make the car look extra cute so that prospective buyers might overlook the missing creature comforts.

Tata's calculation was that as many as 2 million of the 7 million people in India who currently had two wheels would trade up to four wheels. And their market research showed that even at such a low price point, consumers were looking for something more than mere utility. As one villager explained, "If I had a four-wheeler, I would have better marriage prospects in my village."

■ **Will you marry me? The relevant value of your brand can be deeply buried in your consumer's psyche.**

False Prius

Toyota sold a lot of Prius hybrids to consumers who saw saving the planet as reason enough to pay a premium price. As David

Leonhardt wrote in the *New York Times*, the true value of that value may have been less than it appeared to be. For starters, while it is true that hybrids (which basically run on a combination of gas and electricity) get better mileage than nonhybrids, their efficiency is nowhere near as great as the government would have us believe. "In the government's road tests, which are conducted in a world without much traffic or air-conditioning, the Prius gets 55 miles to the gallon. *Consumer Reports* says the car really gets 44 miles to a gallon."

Okay, that's still pretty darn good, but it's only the beginning of the real problem. The heart of the matter is "a government policy that, amazingly enough, seems almost intended to undercut the benefits of efficient cars. In 1978, Congress set a minimum average fuel economy, known as CAFE, for all carmakers." The key word here is *average*. In other words, the nimble Prius, with its high mileage, is averaged with hulking Lexus, with its low mileage, giving Toyota (and other hybrid carmakers) a "free pass . . . to sell a few extra gas guzzlers."

David wrote, "The hybrid, then, is just about the perfect example of what's wrong with our energy policy. It's a Band-Aid that does a lot less to help the earth than we like to tell ourselves." For well-meaning hybrid owners it's "an expensive symbol that they're worried about our planet rather than a true solution."

■ **Value can be more perception than reality, but relevant brands live only in the real world.**

The Green Team

The imperative to stand for something larger than just the brand itself has created awkward situations for some brands, particularly those in the petroleum business. However, Ann Hand, the former senior vice president of global brand marketing innovation for BP, didn't see it that way. While it may seem counterintuitive for a company in the petroleum business to position itself as "environmentally friendly," Ann saw a golden opportunity.

"It is hard to be in the category called 'oil companies,'" she told me in mid-2007, "but it doesn't occur to me that I should therefore not do the right thing. It's just one more obstacle that makes the fight a little more interesting." She added, "It's hard to think about how to take a low-involvement category and be the group that tries to break out and make it high involvement. That's quite a big hill to climb—maybe an impossible hill to climb. But that's my job."

As I spoke with Ann, I began to realize that for her the issue wasn't just about building a perception that BP is more environmentally friendly than its competitors. It had just as much to do with changing the perception that buying gasoline was a drag, a well-known drag.

"I am determined to try to crack the code on gas stations because getting gas has turned into a dreaded experience," she said. "People go to gas stations out of necessity, and they're locked there for three minutes quite unhappily. They usually aren't thrilled about the price of the gas, and they aren't expecting the friendliest of service or the highest quality of food." The solution, she said, was not to attempt to blow up the gas-buying experience and start over again from scratch. The idea was simply to try to make buying gas just a little better than expected.

"In a category where people expect so little, a little better might just mean a lot," she said. "Our hope is that people will drive an extra block or cut across a little bit of extra traffic to choose BP stations because they like what we stand for." That idea manifested itself in BP's slogan, "A Little Better," but more important it paid off on the promise of the advertising by delivering value where it really made a difference—at the pump.

How much difference did Ann Hand think she could make? After admitting that maybe she was "a bit too romantic," she noted that "gas stations once had a positive image of service." She added, "The notion of just accepting that somehow we've gotten into this place where we're part of an industry that has negative perceptions and that we're just going to sit here and take it doesn't feel right."

■ **Adding even just a *little* extra value can make a relevant difference.**

iPod Math

Apple certainly deserves credit for adding value by adding style. But the thing that is often obscured is that style alone does not explain the brand's success. Underneath the hip and sleek veneer of all those iPods, iPhones, and MacBooks is a design with a functionality that in most ways blows away the competition. Hal R. Varian, the economist, wrote an interesting analysis in the *New York Times* of the elements of the iPod and deconstructed where the value really resides. The iPod may be an icon of consumer electronics, but the fact is that it's really just 451 generic parts provided and assembled by a whole bunch of companies in a whole bunch of countries.

A trio of University of California researchers "tried to calculate the value added at different stages of the production process and then assigned that value to the country where the value was created." This was not a simple matter, but guess what? Even though so much of the iPod is made elsewhere, "$163 of the iPod's retail value in the United States was captured by American companies and workers, breaking it down to $75 for distribution and retail costs, $80 to Apple, and $8 to various domestic component makers. . . . The real value of the iPod doesn't lie in its parts or even in putting those parts together. The bulk of the iPod's value is in the conception and design of the iPod."

Apple "may not make the iPod, but they created it. In the end, that's what really matters."

■ **A brand's value is not in its component parts. It's in the creative energy that adds up to a relevant brand experience.**

Unintended Consequences

Apple's reputation for adding value through better design, both aesthetic and functional, is not perfect, however. Yes, the exquisitely designed iPod lets us listen to whatever we want, whenever we want. It is the coolest-looking electronic device on the planet.

As everybody knows, Apple won't let us do what is ultimately the most important thing. It won't let us easily change the damn battery when our iPods die. Why? Because making the battery easily changeable might interrupt the iPod's beautifully seamless contours (more cynically, it might also interfere with Apple's schedule of new product introductions).

Sadly, it took a class-action suit by angry iPod owners before Apple finally agreed to offer a battery replacement service for $65.95 plus tax. You still can't change your own battery (you have to ship your iPod back to Apple), but at least now it can be replaced.

It is equally painful to talk about the soft underbelly of one of my favorite enterprises, Netflix. Like Apple, Netflix is nearly impossible not to like because it put an end to the many aggravating aspects of renting movies from Blockbuster. Sorry to say, one of the key features that made Netflix so appealing—its "unlimited rentals" policy—ultimately was exposed as its Achilles heel.

The famous Netflix promise is that you can rent as many movies as you want each month for a flat fee. Well, not exactly. Netflix acknowledged that it slowed down the rate at which it filled the orders of its heaviest users, a practice critics called "throttling." As with Apple, it took a class-action lawsuit before Netflix would publicly acknowledge that it is giving preferential treatment to its newest and least loyal customers. The strategy presumably is designed both to protect profits and to stimulate Netflix's growth.

A strategy that punishes one's most loyal consumers is hardly sustainable. Wal-Mart's John Fleming certainly saw it that way: "Our challenge is managing our size while staying close to the customers," he told me. "It's about keeping that relationship with the customer in the local communities and cultivating that." Those are words to live by, whether or not Wal-Mart itself always lives up to them.

At the very least, both Apple and Netflix were guilty of undermining their own word-of-mouth marketing strategies. It is just a little weird that these companies, both of which are built on the kind of "evangelism" that most marketers would kill to have, seem oblivious to the fact that buzz can cut both ways. It feels like arrogance, which is not exactly a fundamental principle of relevant marketing.

In neither of these cases is the "soft underbelly" likely to be the company's undoing. Yes, we still love Apple and Netflix, even though they've let us down in significant ways. That enduring loyalty speaks to the relative strengths of the value propositions of each of these companies, which clearly outweigh their relative weaknesses. But their stories also speak to the big risks inherent in big ideas as well as the importance of sensitivity in dealing with the negatives that can be the unintended consequences of otherwise brilliant marketing strategies. Both Netflix and Apple are reacting by taking for granted—and alienating—the very consumers who are at the heart of their successes.

■ **Relevant brands never take their customers for granted.**

Costco Confusion

"Under the high ceilings and bright lights of a warehouse, surrounded by cans of Spam and bags of rice piled to the ceiling, everything looks as if it must be a good deal," wrote David Leonhardt in the *New York Times*. But all is not always as it seems at your local Costco or Sam's Club. Sure, some items clearly are a bargain, but other items not-so-clearly maybe are not. David cited the case of razor blades, and found that you actually can get them a lot cheaper online, at razorsdirect.com, than at Costco—including shipping and without Costco's $50 a year membership fee.

It is precisely that ability to compare prices across channels—"perfect information," as economists call it—that leads shoppers to believe they are making informed choices. It has also driven retailers to "make nearly everything they sell appear to be a bargain," whether it is or it isn't.

The reality is that all this information has not necessarily made us smarter shoppers or even more price sensitive. Even though we have all the information, we can really focus on only one thing, and that one thing tends to be a distraction. At Costco "the very size of the product is the distraction." If it's that big at that price, it must be a bargain, right? Well, maybe not after you factor in the membership fee or that people "eat more of a food item bought in bulk, simply because it's sitting around the kitchen. . . . Then there are the extra shopping trips that Costco customers must make, because many items aren't sold there."

As David Leonhardt wrote, "Let's just call it what it is: not bargain hunting, but entertainment." And the real point is, it's the entertainment value that shoppers love about Costco.

■ **The value of a brand may not always be what it seems, but it is always what is relevant.**

Costco Mojo

"I always buy stuff I don't exactly need," said Ted Reisdorf, commenting on what happens when he shops at Costco, reported by Julie Bick in the *New York Times*. "We always come out with too much," echoed Linda Curtis Schneider, another Costco shopper.

But what may seem like impulsive behavior by Ted and

Linda actually is a carefully laid plan by Costco, the warehouse retailer. One part of that plan is to sell items in bulk. Another is to emphasize high-demand items such as iPods. Yet another part is to let shoppers know that the bargain probably won't be there the next time they shop at Costco, "the largest player in the warehouse market"—even bigger than Wal-Mart's Sam's Club stores.

Most regular shoppers are so conditioned to Costco's merchandising patterns that they typically blame themselves and not Costco if they miss out on a bargain. Shoulda bought it last time!

As Costco senior vice president Joel Benoliel explained, "We'll always have the same staples—the cereal, the detergent—and then we add the 'wow' items."

Not every shopper is so in love with the Costco experience, and many balk at buying in bulk.

"How many things do you need forty-two of, really?" said Teri Franklin, who finds the Costco format wasteful. Costco is not for Teri, but plenty of others are willing to cough up $50 for an annual membership fee—which is actually where Costco earns most of its profits. It also feeds into impulse purchasing because people want to make sure they're getting their money's worth out of their memberships.

"People laughed at the idea of charging someone to shop at your warehouse, but our membership fees are north of $1 billion a year," said Joel. Founded with a single store in Seattle in

1983, Costco has more than five hundred locations worldwide "and finished the 2006 fiscal year with its highest-ever sales, $58.96 billion."

■ **Relevant brands let their customers define their value.**

Trader Joe Secrets

"No one except us knows all the parts of the operation," said Matt Sloan, vice president of merchandising for Trader Joe's, as quoted by Julia Moskin in the *New York Times*. "In that way it's like a conspiracy."

What we do know about Trader Joe's is that it "is radically different in many ways from other food stores," observed Steve Dowdell of *Progressive Grocer* magazine. "The stores are small. They don't rely on national brands. You can't do price comparisons. And they definitely don't offer one-stop shopping. But every product has a story." For example, the tiramisu that Trader Joe's mass-produces, freezes, exports, and sells for $6.99 is based on a recipe from "a small restaurant on the Amalfi coast of Italy." That kind of story is typical for Trader Joe's.

The retailer employs fifteen "category leaders" who "perpetually travel the world visiting all kinds of food businesses—restaurants, farmers' markets, artisanal pasta makers, street stalls, and supermarkets—and then translate their finds into the stores." The process involves an all-important "tasting panel, . . . most well into their forties," who scrutinize every proposed new product. It's a tough room. "Getting the panel's approval can take months, even years." But as Doug Rauch, the president, explained, "The tasting panel is what takes us from having good products to having addictive products."

That is a long way from where Trader Joe's was in the 1960s when it was going out of business trying to compete against 7-Eleven. Things started to turn around when they "stopped selling things like Twinkies . . . and focused on food and wine." Founder Joe Coulombe explained, "We decided . . . to appeal to people who are well educated, well traveled, and underpaid." Today, Trader Joe's has 250 stores, each carrying approximately three thousand items (versus about fifty-five thousand in a typical supermarket). And the focus is on "speed scratch" cooking, as Doug Rauch called it. "Trader Joe's customers are people who really care about cooking but . . . don't have time to chop all the vegetables, cook the chicken, and make the dessert. . . . The whole food business is now trying to figure out how to keep people cooking. . . . We pull in things from all over the world that work for our customers."

And, yes, everything is value priced: "This sounds crazy," said one shopper, "but you feel like this company likes food more than they like money. . . . You don't feel that at the supermarket."

■ **Trader Joe's aligns its value with price as well as with
what's relevant to the lifestyles of its shoppers.**

Disney Relationship Magic

Before joining Disney in 2000, Tom Boyles had a career in
banking, most of it in marketing. He was also what you might
call a "Disneyphile." Basically, that means he vacationed at
Disney for the first time about twenty years ago and then returned at least once a year every year after that. So when a col-
league told him that Disney was looking for someone to head
its customer relationship management (CRM) initiative, Tom
not only jumped at the chance but also had a pretty good idea
of where to start.

As Tom recalled, "When Disney asked me what CRM meant,
I said, 'Well, part of it is knowing your guests well enough to be
relevant to them.' Then I said, 'I've been coming here with my
family every year for more than twenty years, but you all don't
really know who I am."

Six years later Disney not only knows guests like Tom and
his family and how often they have visited but also everyone
who dreams of having a perfect holiday at the Magic Kingdom.
That's a big challenge when you consider that half of all the
households in America are potential visitors. But Disney, said
Tom, is getting it right by investing in the vision and, above all,
letting its customers manage the relationship.

What that comes down to, Tom said, is "knowing the guest well enough, at any given point in time, to know what to do next." What does that really mean? Here's how Tom explained it:

> *In some cases knowing what to do next can mean knowing to do nothing at all. Or it can mean pointing out to the guest the best experiences for their three-year-old, a new attraction, what's changed since their last visit, or which package works best for the entire family.*
>
> *If you buy into the premise that the customers are really managing more and more of the interactions you have with them, then you have to get it right as often as you can, particularly when they contact you.*
>
> *So the idea of "know me and be relevant" really plays out pretty strongly in terms of whether or not they're going to open up the emails that you're sending them as well as when and how they're going to choose to contact you on their own.*

As Tom saw it, that level of relevance is "make or break" for brands. "You can probably get away with not being relevant for maybe a few more years. But I would argue that in another five years—and certainly another ten years—you had better understand what your consumers want from you. You had better understand when you need to push things to consumers and when you need to let them pull it from you."

■ **Knowing what to do next—including doing nothing, when appropriate—is how Disney defines value and maintains its relevance.**

A Rising Tide

Tide detergent may be more than sixty years old, but it is still one of Procter & Gamble's largest and fastest-growing brands. The reason, according to Jim Stengel, P&G's chief marketing officer, is that Tide respects its consumers.

As he told Geoffrey Colvin in an interview for *Fortune* magazine, consumers continue to respond to Tide because "they want to trust something. They want to be understood, they want to be respected, they want to be listened to. They don't want to be talked to. . . . People really do care about the values of a brand and the values of a company." He added, "Businesses and brands that are breaking records are those that inspire trust and affection and loyalty by being authentic, by not being arrogant, and by being empathetic to those they serve."

For example, Pampers went "from being about dryness to being about helping Mom with her baby's development." Said Jim, "It all begins with this idea that we want to make life better. . . . We don't accept that there are any commodity categories," he adds, citing the success of Charmin and Bounty in a "commodity" category like paper goods.

The bottom line, said Jim, is that "marketing is at the center of the company. . . . I wouldn't be sitting here six years into this job if our equities weren't stronger, our innovation pipeline wasn't stronger, our organization wasn't stronger. Those are the kinds of things a CMO needs to be accountable for and should be measured on."

■ Creating trust, understanding, affection, and empathy, and helping people live better—those are the elements of relevance for Procter & Gamble.

PART III

■

Relevant Outcomes

CHAPTER 10

Growth

Zen-Master Profits

At Patagonia, profit is not the goal because
as the Zen master would say, profits happen
when you do everything else right.

—YVON CHOUINARD

G o ahead and call Yvon Chouinard a crazy man. The
feeling probably is mutual. After all, as Susan Casey
reported in *Fortune* magazine, Yvon is someone who
thinks "the average suit ranks somewhere between alcoholic
and criminal on the respect scale," and he compares the un-
sustainable aspirations of American business to "an out-of-
control tumor."

Yvon can get away with saying things like that as long as
his company, Patagonia, keeps on growing—and it has since
he founded it "from the back of his car" in the 1950s. His interest then was simply to support himself by creating better
equipment for mountain climbers than was available on the
market at the time. His goal effectively has not changed since.

His first product was a reusable piton (the metal spikes hammered into rocks to secure ropes for mountain climbing). Before Yvon came along, pitons were left behind; he thought that was not only wasteful but also not great for the environment.

It wasn't until twenty years later, when his enterprise—originally known as Chouinard Equipment—had grown into America's largest maker of climbing equipment, that Yvon fully realized he had become a businessman. Some might question that.

What kind of businessman would let his staff leave for the beach when the surf is up? Yvon Chouinard encourages it because he believes that blurring the lines between work and play is good for business.

What kind of businessman would shift 50 percent of his production into a brand-new category in which it has no credibility? Yvon Chouinard has done it because he believes global warming will eventually destroy Patagonia's base business in cold weather sports. So Patagonia is now in the water sports business. "We're getting into the surf market," he explained to *Fortune* magazine, "because it's never going to snow again, and the waves are going to get bigger and bigger."

Think about it: One of the business world's most celebrated environmentalists is changing his business model based on an assumption that the planet is melting. His insanely honest premise is remarkable not only because it is so astonishing but also because nobody doubts for a moment that he really, truly means it. The degree of authenticity here is profound and breathtaking.

Then again, he could be just a crazy man.

How's It Growing?

For a somewhat less lofty view, I asked one of Yvon Chouinard's people, Rick Ridgeway, Patagonia's president of communications, to outline his perspective on the key growth drivers for the organization. I put the same question to some folks from GlaxoSmithKline, Dunkin' Donuts, and Meridian Consulting Group.

Rick Ridgeway, Patagonia

We manage our growth very carefully. It has always been organic, and it will continue to be. Consequently, we're seldom looking to broaden our distribution because we feel it would get us into areas where the brand doesn't belong. We're also unique in our own industry in having essentially five channels of distribution.

We have our own retail stores and our own mail order, catalog sales. We also have our own online sales as well as very robust wholesale distribution in addition to very robust direct distribution to pro athletes and key influencers. We can't grow the business at a really high double-digit rate and keep all those channels happy and healthy. So, acquiring new customers within existing channels is our focus.

Donna Sturgess, GlaxoSmithKline

The greatest key driver of growth at GlaxoSmithKline is that we have taken innovation on board as an organizing principle. We have identified innovation as our greatest opportunity to drive growth in the consumer division, and we have aligned our structure, operations, resources, and budgets accordingly.

Taking cost and complexity out of the organization is a subset of our growth strategy; the money that is saved is then plowed back into the business. It really is the ultimate in portfolio management. We are taking costs out to fuel innovation and creating our own internal cycle to manage our business based on what is best for the portfolio in total.

John Gilbert, formerly of Dunkin' Donuts
(currently of TJX Companies)

For Dunkin' Donuts the shift from at-home coffee to on-the-go coffee has been a tremendous catalyst for growth. In addition, the Echo Boomer generation is now entering its formative coffee-drinking years. They are starting to get their first jobs and starting to drink coffee. The difference is that it's not Folger's at home. It's Dunkin' on the road. That is probably the biggest engine.

The next biggest engine is related but not quite the same. The way consumers use beverages today is so different from the past. In contemporary marketplaces, beverages have to do something extra for you. Orange juice might be "immune fortified," for example; it can't be just orange juice anymore. That trend is providing tremendous interest in our beverage products.

A third engine is fragmentation, which is both an opportunity and a threat. The opportunity is that consumers increasingly are accessing brands and brand information through the Internet and local retail, and decreasingly through big-brand advertising. That may be a threat if you're in the big-brand advertising business—which we are to some degree—but it's also a growth opportunity if you can target your products specifically for a particular consumer or occasion.

Michael Shinall, Meridian

Retailers should do two things to drive growth, which almost sound contradictory. One is, they need to figure out exactly which businesses they're in so that they can focus better on those businesses. At the same time they need to experiment with new businesses and determine whether there are new growth opportunities for them.

Most manufacturers, meanwhile, have a significant productivity problem in that they used to sell about a million dollars' worth of merchandise with one hundred items; today they'll sell $2 million worth but with one thousand items. They are getting growth but at the expense of productivity. So, while manufacturers do need to think about item rationalization, they also need to think hard about what really constitutes innovation because new products are a key growth driver.

Googlenomics

Google's strategy of making serial acquisitions may not be the best way to achieve its growth objectives. That is the opinion of Chris Zook of Bain & Company, writing in the *Wall Street Journal*.

It is possible that everything could work out for Google in the end, but the odds, said Chris, are against it. "The success rate for major, life-changing mergers is only about one in ten," he said. "It is less than one in seven for moves into a hot new market far from the company's core." The better approach, said Chris, author of *Beyond the Core*, is to mine "hidden assets" that an enterprise already possesses but has "failed to tap for maximum growth potential." The better example, he said, is (yawn) Apple.

"The iPod drew on the company's well-known skills in software, user-friendly product design, and imaginative marketing—all underexplored capabilities." Samsung, meanwhile, redefined its core by selling or shutting down a total of seventy-six businesses, "freeing up resources to invest in its lagging but promising semiconductor and consumer electronics businesses."

Chris said that Bain conducted a "three-year study of transformation," revealing that "assets yielding the best results are usually camouflaged as hidden business platforms, untapped customer insights, and underused capabilities."

GE "revitalized itself via GE Capital, a division that has now fueled its parents' growth and profitability for years." Nestlé "created the core of a new multibillion-dollar business" by recombining "a number of isolated food and drink products" into Nestlé Food Services.

Harmon International, the audio equipment maker, increased its market value fortyfold over twelve years based on the simple insight that "customers who bought expensive equipment at home were spending more time in their cars."

So now Harmon is big into "high-end automotive 'infotainment' systems." Finally, noted Chris, "more than 50 percent of the companies in the Global 500 have seen their world changed by threats to their core business models." The best response, he said, "is actually right in front of them, hidden from view."

■ **Relevance, my friend, means Googling from within.**

Apple Scruffs

It may comfort some (and traumatize others) to learn that even Apple isn't perfect—at least when it comes to the kind of relevance that ultimately drives growth. Yes, Apple's iPod franchise effectively owns the market for MP3 players and keeps feeding that frenzy with a steady progression of newer and cooler models. In that regard, Apple seems to know no direction other than up.

Let's not forget, however, that Apple's original business—personal computers—is anything but a growth engine, mired as it is at somewhere between a 2 or 3 percent share of the market. That is down considerably from Apple's 1984 peak of around 14 percent. It is even more important to understand why that is—and the reason can be summed up in a single word: distribution. While much of the world (including me) is in awe of Apple's stores, the fact remains that as of late 2007 there were only 185 of them.

Hewlett-Packard, meanwhile, was being distributed through twenty-three thousand stores, as noted in a *New York Times* article by Randall Stross. True enough, you could buy an Apple at Best Buy and other retail locations (although Apple does not disclose how many). You could buy one online, too. But chances were that if you were thinking about switching to an Apple Macintosh from a Windows box, you would have difficulty finding one to try before you buy. Until Apple figures out a way to get more of its hardware into stores where people could experience them firsthand, it is highly unlikely they will grow out of single digits in market share.

■ **When it comes to growth, relevance is distribution, distribution, distribution.**

Lowe's Versus Home Depot

Most shoppers prefer Lowe's to Home Depot, but they spend more money with Home Depot simply because its stores are more convenient, reported Mary Ellen Lloyd in the *Wall Street Journal*.

A 2007 survey of one thousand consumers by Consumer Specialists found that 53 percent preferred Lowe's, compared to 47 percent for Home Depot. Consumers rated Lowe's "higher than Home Depot in most areas, including product selection and customer service." In fact, Lowe's widened its favorability rating over Home Depot from "a 51 percent to 49 percent preference" in a similar survey conducted in 2006. However, in one key area, convenience, Lowe's lost its edge. At the time, Home Depot had just 2,206 stores nationwide, compared to 1,400 Lowe's locations. Fred Miller, president of Consumer Specialists, said Home Depot's greater number of locations makes all the difference. "If you're going to win only one [category], that's a good one to win," he said. As a result, those who preferred Home Depot said they spent an average of $763 there over the previous six months, compared to $322 at Lowe's. Those who preferred Lowe's reported spending $604 there, compared to $454 at Home Depot.

Lowe's planned to open more stores (150 to 170 in fiscal 2007), and Home Depot said it would spend $2.2 billion that same year to improve its shopping experience. Geographically, Lowe's had its edge in the South, while Home Depot led in the Midwest and West. Demographically, women liked Lowe's by a margin of 54 percent to 46 percent.

■ **When it comes to growth, 80 percent of relevance is just showing up (my apologies to Woody Allen).**

More Starbucks

A key impediment to Starbucks's growth, as it took aim at tripling its number of stores, was that some locals objected to the Starbucksification of their neighborhoods. As reported by Janet Adamy in the *Wall Street Journal*, one Denver neighborhood landlord even asked Starbucks "to replace its standard green-and-white mermaid logo sign with something more original." Starbucks came up with "a brushed stainless steel coffee cup to adorn the store."

To be fair, Starbucks generally tried to make its stores fit in with their environs but traditionally used "four coffee-inspired motifs that used similar earth tones and plush over-sized furniture. . . . Then [in 2005] Starbucks switched from the coffee motifs to three more sophisticated decorative platforms with a broader array of colors, tiles, furniture, and artwork." The new palettes were "Classico, a European decor scheme with rich woods that recalls an old coffeehouse; the di Moda, a sleek, urban platform with sharp-edged elements; and the Origins, a brightly colored scheme with bamboo touches that evokes a Moroccan bazaar." All the newer designs featured "open shelving behind the bars" that evoked "the mercantile feel of Starbucks's first-ever location in Seattle's Pike Place Market."

To make sure they got it right in each neighborhood, Starbucks actually deployed designers into regional offices, according to Launi Skinner, senior vice president of store development for Starbucks. The retailer also took special care to preserve key elements as well as the more subtle touches of the vintage buildings it occupied, such as the fireplace mantel in a limestone building in Chicago's Beverly neighborhood.

Not everyone was impressed. "It will still be too sterile and too perfect, too institutionalized," said Xtine Hanson of delocator.net fame. But Starbucks patron Jim Venckus noticed the difference at the Beverly Starbucks and liked it. "Mostly they're just large rooms with a counter," he said, referring to other Starbucks stores. "I think the designer or architect put a lot of thought into this."

■ **The "grande" plan for growth at Starbucks was to look more relevant locally while building more stores globally.**

Staples staples

The staple of growth for Staples was a better shopping experience, which resulted in an 18 percent increase in profits, to $834 million, in 2005, reported Michael Myser in *Business 2.0*.

"Customers wanted an easier shopping experience," said Shira Goodman, executive vice president of marketing for Staples, explaining a focus-group revelation. "It became clear that's where the opportunities were." That epiphany arrived in 2001 when Staples was hurting and its customers were complaining; in fact, the "ratio of complaints to kudos at Staples stores in 2001" was 8:1. That led to a second lightbulb moment; that all the advertising in the world would be for naught unless it paid off in the real world, inside Staples stores. According to research, the main thing customers expected was to find what they wanted—"a simple, straightforward shopping experience." Shira said, "They wanted knowledgeable and helpful associates and hassle-free shopping." Prices were secondary.

Shira started by removing "some eight hundred superfluous items, such as Britney Spears backpacks." She also "added larger signs and retrained sales associates to walk shoppers to the correct aisle. Since customers revealed that the availability of ink was one of their biggest concerns, the company introduced an in-stock guarantee on printer cartridges. . . . It took about a year to get the stores up to snuff." Only then did Staples introduce "That Was Easy," its advertising campaign, which boasted something like 70 percent recall among consumers.

One more tip from Shira Goodman: Take the long view. "We set clear expectations that this would be a three- or five-year journey," she said, adding, "We're in the early stages of what can be a very strong retail brand and message."

■ **"That Was Easy" was the Staples ad slogan, but achieving growth involved the hard work of creating a more relevant shopping experience.**

Just One Thing

Relevance is all about simplicity; in many cases it is just one thing that makes the difference.

Porsche Economics

Compared to the 911 Turbo, the Porsche Carrera GT handled only slightly better and accelerated faster by just two-tenths of a second, but it was priced at "almost four times" as much, wrote Robert H. Frank in the *New York Times*. The reason, said Robert, was this: "People who really care about cars find these small improvements genuinely exciting." And they will pay through the tailpipe for them.

Birkenstock Culture

What was it about Birkenstock sandals that kept them growing at a steady 10 percent a year, year after year, since 1966?

Scott Radcliffe, marketing director for Birkenstock, said he thought the appeal was cultural. As he told the *New York Times*, "Birkenstock fans . . . feel like they're part of something bigger than other shoe choices, frankly." Most often that "something bigger" was an enduring association with "granola-crunching, Volvo-driving, fill-in-the-blank stereotypes."

T.G.I. Traffic

By cutting both the sizes of its portions and the prices of its food, T.G.I. Fridays attracted "more customers and perhaps bigger profits," reported Andrew Martin in the *New York Times*. Over a four-month test period "the number of customers increased . . . by 1.4 percent, compared with the same period a year earlier. For the entire casual-dining industry, guest counts were down by 2.8 percent during that period."

Bobcat City

By keeping its factories at home in North Dakota instead of outsourcing overseas, Bobcat, makers of farm machinery, achieved steady growth—11 percent a year for ten years, reported Timothy Aeppel in the *Wall Street Journal*. What Bobcat may have lost in cost savings it seemed to more than make up in the kind of innovation that comes when folks live and work together, and design and build tools for their friends and neighbors. Not only did Bobcat's approach result in superior new products, but it made the company North Dakota's largest exporter. Its "made here" position also gave Bobcat an edge over foreign competitors here at home.

Virgin Turf

Virgin Atlantic may have flown only thirty-seven planes, but it punched above its weight, in part because it put "a huge amount of capacity in the market," said Steve Ridgway, CEO, in a *Wall Street Journal* interview with Daniel Michaels.

"We only fly big twin-aisle aircraft," he explained. That added up to more than "five million passengers, which was not to be sneered at," he said. Then there was all the other stuff Virgin Group did "from music stores to cola to cell phones—all presented with an air of hipness and iconoclasm." Then, of course, there was Sir Richard Branson's "persona," which tended to attract extra notice and on a global basis.

But perhaps more than anything, the key to Virgin's success was what Steve called "the revolution—we put the customer at the heart of the business. That wasn't how airlines were run historically. They were run by operational people who didn't really like passengers because they turned up late and dropped peanuts everywhere." Virgin's customer focus led to innovations that Steve said were based on "the value proposition and what people will pay for. Our single biggest innovation was always to try to wrong-foot the market," he said. "We've always positioned our products as a notch out of the convention."

Most notable was Virgin's offering first-class service at business-class prices, and something close to business-class service at economy prices. "We were the first airline to be completely egalitarian ten years before anyone else put seat-back video in all cabins—it wasn't just for the beautiful people at the front of the plane."

He added, "We also have confidence about doing things that consumers probably wouldn't recognize they want until they see it." For example, he said, focus groups were asked if they wanted their Club Houses to offer haircuts and shoeshines. The focus groups said no, but Virgin decided to offer the services anyway. "And they all went 'Oh, wow—this is great.'"

- **Relevant brands grow because they *like* their customers and understand them well enough to predict what they want.**

Dare to Be Different

Growth may seem to come easily to the "usual suspects"— companies such as Apple, Google, and Procter & Gamble, for example. Less well known are the growth strategies of companies like Rolls-Royce and DeWALT. You might not expect these old-line companies to be home to relevant growth strategies, but by looking beyond the status quo these businesses discovered ways to boost returns. Each of the following growth stories offers different and compelling insights into how to create growth where stagnation might otherwise prevail.

Rolls-Royce

We're not talking about Rolls-Royce motorcars but, rather, the aircraft engine business—Rolls-Royce Group—which has been run by the British government since the 1970s. It is actually only relatively recently, under the leadership of CEO John Rose, that Rolls-Royce grew from just about a dead stop to become the second largest manufacturer of aircraft engines behind General Electric.

Rolls got there in part by creating what *BusinessWeek* called "one of the world's most sophisticated help desks," which "continuously monitors the health of some 3,000 engines for 45 airline customers." In addition, because its service guarantee is so comprehensive, Rolls became more focused than ever on making sure the engines didn't fail in the first place.

As a result, Rolls-Royce won 86 percent of orders for the Boeing 787 and split Airbus A380 orders with GE. According to analyst Sandy Morris of ABN Amro, Rolls-Royce Group was poised to enjoy a 65 percent year-on-year increase in operating profits in 2005, while investors bid up the stock 46 percent by early 2006.

DeWALT

According to an article in *Fortune* magazine, DeWALT, the power tools marketer, grew to become "one of Black & Decker's most profitable divisions." That was quite something for a brand that was pretty much dead until the marketing team at DeWALT discovered that the brand still had plenty of juice left among professional builders. The growth driver for DeWALT actually was a very specific consumer insight. Dan Gregory, DeWALT's VP of marketing, commented, "The contractor doesn't want a tool that has the same name as his wife's toaster."

That kind of insight was critical because at the time professionals accounted for about 69 percent of all tool sales in the United States. DeWALT played up its reputation as "more rugged and reliable" and parlayed its reinvigorated image into $1 billion in annual sales and a 35 percent share of the professional tool market.

Crack Team USA

No discussion about unconventional approaches to growth would be complete without mentioning the incredible success of a St. Louis–based company whose business is basement repair. It is hard to imagine a more mundane commodity business than fixing cracks in concrete. Realizing this, the company's president, Bob Kodner, got the idea that maybe a little comic relief would help sell his ostensibly dull product.

As reported by Gwendolyn Bounds in the *Wall Street Journal*, Bob "imagined a logo featuring a cartoonish, smiling gray piece of cement with feet and hands and a crack running down his head." He had his cousin design the logo, which he dubbed "Mr. Happy Crack," and plastered it on thirty-four St. Louis buses. Suddenly the phones started ringing with people wanting to know if they could get a T-shirt or a hat with "Mr. Happy Crack" on it.

Soon after, Bob's company had ten offices in eight states and was projecting as many as 150 in North America by the end of 2007. He credited his logo with winning over potential franchisees, and his franchisees credited the logo with winning over customers. Revenues from the sales of T-shirts and other paraphernalia alone accounted for about 5 percent of the company's revenues, which totaled $10 million as of 2006.

■ **Relevant brands think about and then reignite what their consumers truly want and have the courage to cut a new path.**

Jump the Shark

Quoting Woody Allen again, in *Annie Hall,* "A relationship . . . is like a shark. . . . It has to constantly move forward or it dies. And I think what we got on our hands is a dead shark." Getting growth means staying relevant, and staying relevant means always moving forward. It means always changing to keep up with what's relevant. That's not easy for anyone, from the smallest entrepreneur to the largest organization. Seeking wisdom on the subject, I once again turned to Rick Ridgeway of Patagonia, Donna Sturgess of GlaxoSmithKline, John

Gilbert, then at Dunkin' Donuts, and Michael Shinall of Meridian Consulting Group for their best advice. How must a marketing organization change to achieve growth?

Rick Ridgeway, Patagonia

Our goal at Patagonia is to synchronize all our marketing efforts across all channels so that all channels speak with a common voice. Even more important, they must all speak in support of one another. For example, because more than 70 percent of our customers who receive our catalogs actually make their purchases online, we need to make sure that our catalog and Web groups are working well together.

Our company is horizontal and has a culture of collaboration. That can slow us down a bit sometimes, but when we make decisions, we have buy-in across the company. We also have the advantage of doing everything ourselves. We have our own in-house ad agency, our own in-house design department, and our in-house Internet department for the Web site. We don't even have a marketing department per se. Rather, we have people who coordinate the marketing that is done in all these various areas of the company.

Donna Sturgess, GSK

Where in the past we drove a lot of our business based on analytical excellence, we are evolving our organization to where it has equal parts of analysis and innovation. We don't want big crazy ideas that don't make financial sense. The point is, innovation has to be a manifestation of a strategy. Otherwise, you might have wonderful ideas that in the short term make a lot of money but in the long term don't provide a platform for growth.

I'm also a believer that ideas can erupt from anywhere. The question is, are you there to catch the ideas? Ideas travel along the path of least resistance. Someone who sits in a central marketing group should be able to grasp the next big idea for Target, for example. But you want to make sure that someone working out in the market who has a great idea about what should happen at Target also knows whom to direct that to. Ideas should be able to travel in both directions.

John Gilbert, formerly of Dunkin' Donuts (currently of TJX)

There will still be a need for classic brand management. There will still be a need for teams of people identifying and satisfying consumer needs. But how we express the solutions to those needs will change fairly substantially.

Already something like 95 percent of TiVo owners opt out of TV commercials. There are a lot of things we're trying to do to compensate for that, but for now it comes down to the law of large numbers, and TV gets you big audiences quickly, efficiently, and cost effectively. The problem is that there's no substitute for the impact we feel on our business today from TV.

Michael Shinall, Meridian

We've seen organizations succeed in a number of ways, but one model that is increasingly emerging is to create a stand-alone innovation division with defined processes, hurdle rates, and time dimensions associated with bringing new products to market. The innovation function can be very successful because its sole focus is on developing brands, not building them. Then, at some point, after a new product has gone to market and met a certain level of success, it is integrated within the brand team itself.

A key difference is that today there's a third head that is often consulted: the retailer. Previously, new product development was based on a balance between what the consumer wanted and what was profitable. Innovation ten to fifteen years ago typically meant marketing innovation, such as packaging product and positioning. It's critical to have a sales or retailer perspective of new product innovation.

Chipotle Integrity

Its burritos might cost too much and its lines could be too long, but Chipotle Mexican Grill has still managed to become "arguably the most successful fast-food chain in recent years," reported Janet Adamy in the *Wall Street Journal*.

Chipotle got there mainly "by rejecting almost every major technique on which the industry was built. . . . it doesn't advertise on television. It doesn't franchise. It has some of the highest ingredient costs in the industry." Its billboard ads don't even show its products, and its top executives "aren't especially concerned that customers wait as long as ten minutes in lines that routinely stretch out the door."

The chain's founder, Steve Ells, persists in upgrading ingredients and has even started "buying some locally grown peppers, onions, and cilantro, and serving dairy products from 'pasture-raised cows.'" He said he hopes his example "will pressure suppliers to raise animals more naturally . . . an approach he calls 'food with integrity.'" Steve said he realizes he probably cares more about where Chipotle's ingredients come from than do his customers, but then he is an alum of the legendary Culinary Institute of America.

He opened his first Chipotle in Denver back in 1993, initially as a way to make enough money to open a finer restaurant. His idea was to do for quick-serve what Whole Foods had done for supermarkets: "popularize natural foods by selling them in an appealing environment."

In 1998, with fourteen locations, he "sold part of the company to McDonald's," giving the chain a $360 million cash infusion. By 2007, Chipotle had about 670 locations, and it planned to open at least another 130 the following year. Its shares doubled between 2006 and 2007, making it the best performing publicly held U.S. restaurant chain. And while traditional fast-food chains were posting same-store-sales growth in the low single digits, Chipotle increased its same-store sales at a double-digit rate each year for almost a decade.

When I interviewed Jim Adams, Chipotle's executive director of marketing, in early 2008, he was blunt about the secret of

Chipotle's success: "You know," he said, "there's just no excuse to serve crap. There just isn't any. And too many places serve crap."

■ **Even an ostensibly lowly category like fast food can refresh relevance and drive growth based on nothing more than the audacity of integrity.**

Patagonia Dreaming

Yvon Chouinard applied his unusual philosophy of growth to Patagonia's surprising partnership with Wal-Mart. He persuaded Wal-Mart to use less organic cotton and more synthetics, applying the argument that people throw away cotton clothes but synthetics can be recycled. "If Wal-Mart does onetenth of what they say they're going to do, it will be incredible," he said.

He might be right. Wal-Mart certainly is trying to reinvent itself as "environmentally friendly" these days. Wal-Mart may actually be able to make a real difference (especially if it succeeds in its stated goal to motivate 100 million of its shoppers to buy just one compact fluorescent lightbulb). At the very least, Wal-Mart may have been sharing a little too much Kool-Aid with Yvon Chouinard. One hundred million lightbulbs? We'll see if a little bit of insanity is, in fact, an active ingredient of growth for Wal-Mart. The acid test for both companies is whether they deliver.

As for Yvon Chouinard, let's hope he is wrong about global warming. Either way, he'll almost certainly be a winner and continue to grow and be profitable because he is staying relevant to the values that made Patagonia an uncommon success.

■ **Relevant brands are less fixated on short-term marketing return on investment than they are on long-term growth.**

Coda

In the mad rush to turn every digital dot in America into an advertising message, we forgot about the most important thing: *What's the point?*

The point is, if we're not helping people live better lives, we are not helping ourselves.

If all we are doing is interrupting people who don't have time for interruptions, we can't expect their attention.

If all we are doing is annoying people who have zero tolerance for annoyance, we can't earn their trust.

If all we are doing is pelting people with endlessly irrelevant messages, we can't claim their loyalty.

And if we can't claim their loyalty, we don't have a prayer of a positive return on investment.

We can run whatever media-mix model we like, but all we're likely to achieve is a marginal improvement on what is otherwise a downward spiral of failure.

Relevance and success will come to those marketers who are listening more than talking, and delivering more than just advertising.

The medium is no longer the message. It is the promise.

The question is, can we keep it?

Certain Secrets of Relevant Brands

- Relevant brands often find their focus within a key demographic group but do not base their strategies solely on issues of age, gender, ethnicity, or income.
- Relevant brands seek to help people live happier lives but do so by addressing everyday problems, not by pandering to fashionable aspirations.
- Relevant brands may not totally reject advertising but recognize that media-driven communication is less critical to success than delivering a meaningful solution.
- Relevant brands understand that connecting with consumers is no longer as much about sending them a message as it is about hearing their reply.

- Relevant brands see themselves as their own best customers.
- Relevant brands know the difference between wasting money and investing in their consumers.
- Relevant brands are less interested in the whizbang of bells and whistles than in the elegance of simple ideas that work.
- Relevant brands have figured out that retail is not just a distribution channel; it's where experiences are created and sales are made.
- Relevant brands do not define value at the traditional crossroads of price and quality; they create value that really hits home.
- Relevant brands are less fixated on short-term marketing return on investment than they are on long-term growth.

Acknowledgments

This book is dedicated to my father, David X Manners, whose nearly hundred years of life were the picture of relevance. And to my mother, Ruth Ann Manners, who taught me three very important lessons of male relevance: how to cook, sew, and iron.

It is also written, with love, for my wife, Beth, and our kids, Holly and Spencer.

My special thanks to Will Weisser for noticing my work and recommending it to his colleagues at Portfolio: Adrian Zackheim; Jeffrey Krames; my new favorite editor, Adrienne Schultz; her assistant, Brooke Carey; and publicist Maureen Cole. Equally huge thanks to Heath Row, who invited me to write a series of essays for *Fast Company*, which became the basis for this book. Thanks also to Lynne d Johnson and Saabira Chaudhuri of *Fast Company*.

Encouragement is essential to a project like this, which is

why Megan Casey is not only supremely relevant but essential, to boot. It is also safe to say that you would not be reading these words on this page were it not for the remarkable enthusiasm of Seth Godin (who, among other things, introduced me to Lisa DiMona, the world's best literary agent).

One huge, sweeping thanks to all the writers, journalists, and others whose work I read and digest in my daily report, *Cool News of the Day*, to the many brilliant marketers and living legends who have given me interviews for *The Hub*, and to everyone who reads my stuff.

Over the past twenty years I have been fortunate to have clients who are also friends (or maybe it's the other way around), especially Spencer Hapoienu, Al Wittemen, Dori Molitor, Todd Waters, Mike Shinall, Tim Hawkes, Ted Bohnen, Stuart Armstrong, Patrick Meyer, Robin Austin, Bernie Trueblood, Vince Weiner, Kenn Devane, Bill Zengel, Brad Wendkos, Alison Hasbach, and Jon Kramer.

And I'd like to acknowledge two friends in particular, Chris Hoyt and Jeff McElnea, for being (and staying) there from the very beginning of my business life.

Most of all, thanks to my team: Peter F. Eder, Jane H. Manners, Julie E. Manners, Joseph McMahon, John S. Dykes, Chris Winn, Mike Forman, Ric Lopez-Fabrega, Roberta Ferriera, and Bertha Rosenberg.

Last but not least, a heartfelt thanks to Juliet and Manny Dalis, to brothers Jon, Mike, and Paul, and to Philip A. DiCostanzo for remembering the strawberries.

Notes

CHAPTER 1: Demographics

7   **"We don't talk about":** Mike Linton, personal interview, March 2, 2006.

8   **Leslie Kilgore, chief marketing:** Leslie Kilgore, personal interview, December 9, 2005.

8   **Anne Saunders, a former senior:** Anne Saunders, personal interview, September 19 and 23, 2005.

8   **"Thirty or forty years ago":** John Fleming, personal interview, January 4, 2006.

8   **"a demographic profile of":** Paul Latham, personal interview, September 25, 2007.

9   **"Yes—people who eat!":** Jim Adams, personal interview, January 17, 2008.

10   **"Demographics are not discredited":** Larry Flanagan, personal interview, April 6, 2007.

10   **"The consumption behavior across":** Cindy Hennessy, personal interview, April 13, 2007.

10   **"Demographics are a really good":** Ruby Anik, personal interview, April 4, 2007.

11   **"I think demographics are becoming":** Spencer Hapoienu, personal interview, March 24, 2008.

12   **Before Peter Gelb:** Stephanie Clifford, "Dramatic Results," *Inc.* magazine, October 1, 2007.

13   **The Broadway success of *Wicked*:** Campbell Robertson, "Tweens Love Broadway, But Can't Save it Alone," *New York Times*, October 2, 2007.

14   **The producers of *The Color Purple*:** Brookes Barnes, "Color Purple Proves Black Themes Can Make Green on Great White Way," *Wall Street Journal*, December 1, 2006.

16   **Nowhere is this practice more flagrant:** Jeffrey Trachtenberg, "Why Book Industry Sees the World Split Still by Race," *Wall Street Journal*, December 6, 2006.

17   **"A lot of what we do":** Julie Bosman, "Hey, Kid, You Want to Buy a Toyota Scion?" *New York Times*, June 14, 2006.

18   **"There is a growing trend":** Bill Higgins, personal interview, May 16, 2005.

18   **"Financial services are an opportunity":** Chuck McLeish, personal interview, May 19, 2005.

19   **"Health clubs, perhaps":** Perrin Kaplan, personal interview, June 2, 2005.

19   **"The PGA—I've never understood":** Steve Gold, personal interview, April 1, 2005.

20   **That was a 2006 story by Tara Parker-Pope:** Tara Parker-Pope, "Hip Government Exercise Campaign Looks for Its New Move," *Wall Street Journal*, September 6, 2006.

20   **For example, topping a search:** Tara Parker-Pope, "Watching Food Ads on TV May Program Kids to Overeat," *Wall Street Journal*, July 10, 2007.

22   **In fact, there was a great:** Gerri Hirshey, "Local Food 101, with a School as His Lab," *New York Times*, May 13, 2007.

22   **As Alex Williams wrote:** Alex Williams, "Gay by Design, or a Lifestyle Choice?" *New York Times*, April 12, 2007.

24   **According to a *Wall Street Journal* article:** John Lippman, "Mining 'Brokeback Mountain,'" *Wall Street Journal*, January 27, 2006.

25   **American Airlines hit some serious:** Joe Sharkey, "Maybe a Lavender Web Site Wasn't How to Attract Women," *New York Times*, April 17, 2007.

26   **As Tim Mapes, the airline's:** Tim Mapes, "Speed of Song," reveries.com, May 1, 2004.

27   **"The insight is that most":** John Gilbert, personal interview, December 12, 2005.

28   **"Patagonia is not a very demographically":** Rick Ridgeway, personal interview, December 15, 2005.

CHAPTER 2: Aspirations

31   **According to an article:** Karlene Lukovitz, "Product Tips You Can Use, by Way of Cellphone," *New York Times*, April 24, 2007.

32   **As reported by Elizabeth Weise:** "Idea of Simple Life Takes Hold," *USA Today,* March 22, 2006.

33   **Putting shoppers at ease:** "Taking an Emotional Audit of Rodeo Drive," *Wall Street Journal*, November 1, 2007.

35   **It is not that Dockers:** Ray A. Smith, "At Levi Strauss, Dockers Are In," *Wall Street Journal*, February 14, 2007.

36   **As reported by Janet Adamy:** Janet Adamy, "Dunkin' Donuts Tries to Go Upscale, but Not Too Far," *Wall Street Journal*, April 8, 2006.

38   **"We simply want to make sure":** John Fleming, *The Hub*, March-April 2006.

39   **"We are *not* ashamed":** Mindy Fetterman, "J. C. Penney Sells with an Attitude," *USA Today*, March 2, 2006.

40   **But according to an article:** Jeff Bailey, "Where Clean and Friendly Always Work," *New York Times*, September 18, 2006.

41 **When I asked John Riordon:** John Riordon, "Like Airplanes, Like Rugby," reveries.com, November 1, 2002.

41 **Jack Kennard, senior vice president:** Jack Kennard, "Are Your Assets Activated?" reveries.com, November 1, 2004.

42 **"There is a satisfaction":** Alex Kuczynski, "Exploring the Great Indoors, Late at Night," *New York Times*, September 7, 2006.

43 **"Our customers, both on the phone":** Steve Fuller, personal interview, October 24, 2007.

45 **"Brands are made out of excellent":** Scott Deaver, personal interview, September 25, 2007.

45 **"There are four areas":** Ken Fenyo, personal interview, October 27, 2007.

46 **"The simplest and most basic way":** David Gitow, personal interview, October 15, 2007.

46 **"Loyalty is explicitly part":** Eric Leininger, personal interview, October 30, 2007.

47 **"Loyalty is about understanding":** David Norton, personal interview, October 5, 2007.

48 **"These fans—these kids":** Reggie Fils-Aime, personal interview, February 13, 2007.

CHAPTER 3: Advertising

51 **"As a niche, that idea is huge":** Dori Molitor, personal interview, December 11, 2006.

52 **"This is going to seem like a bit":** John Gilbert, *The Hub*, January-February 2006.

53 **Chris Martin, the chief executive:** Chris Martin, "Word of Martin," reveries.com, November 1, 2004.

54 **"While our paid channels":** Leslie Kilgore, *The Hub*, January-February 2006.

55 **"What we are all about":** Anne Saunders, n.p., n.d.

56 **"No. We don't have an advertising":** Paul Latham, *The Hub*, November-December 2007.

57 **As reported in *BusinessWeek*:** "Leader of the Packs," *BusinessWeek*, October 31, 2005.

59 **"The business obviously has been":** Geoffrey Frost, personal interview, August 19, 2005.

61 **It is worth listening:** Jon Fine, "Reworking the Ad Mix," *BusinessWeek*, October 23, 2006.

62 **Intrigued by that comment:** Jim Garrity, personal interview, July 24, 2007.

63 **"The assignment in '95":** Louise Story, "Microsoft's Vista Debut Wasn't Nearly So 'Wow,'" *New York Times*, February 5, 2007.

64 **"We haven't spent":** Peter Engardio, "A Night's Sleep, Ultracheap," *BusinessWeek*, January 23, 2006.

65 **"We were shocked":** Beth Kwon, "Sales More Than Doubled Last Year," *Inc.* magazine, January 2007.

67 **When Dr. Joshua Freedman:** Kenneth Chang, "Enlisting Science's Lessons to Entice More Shoppers to Spend More," *New York Times*, September 29, 2006.

70 **it's awareness, wrote:** Adam Leipzeig, "How to Sell a Movie (or Fail) in Four Hours," *New York Times*, November 13, 2005.

71 **"In a television model":** Donna Sturgess, personal interview, June 24, 2006.

CHAPTER 4: Insights

80 **According to an article:** Brier Dudley, "At KEXP, Technology & Music Embrace," *Seattle Times*, April 30, 2007.

81 **Even more important:** Avi Salzman, "Streaming from a Storefront," *New York Times*, May 21, 2006.

83   **"I tried to pick up on":** Constantine Maroulis, personal interview, June 24, 2006.

85   **As Yahoo!'s Jeff Weiner:** Jeff Weiner, "Blogs Will Change Your Business," *BusinessWeek*, May 2005.

85   **Conversing with your consumers:** Jeff Jarvis, "Dell Learns to Listen," *BusinessWeek*, October 17, 2007.

87   **Indeed, about three-quarters:** "Future of Innovation," *The Economist*, March 10, 2005.

89   **"One thing that I find particularly":** Stephen Berkov, personal interview, December 7, 2006.

89   **"I believe that there's no single":** James S. Figura, personal interview, December 20, 2006.

90   **"We have developed several techniques":** Dori Molitor, *The Hub*, January-February 2007.

90   **The greatest strength:** Jay Greene, "Where Designers Rule," *Business-Week*, November 5, 2007.

92   **Alan George—that's how:** Luisa Kroll, "A Fresh Face," *Forbes*, July 8, 2002.

93   **According to an article:** Emilie Boyer King, "All the News That's Kid Friendly," *Christian Science Monitor*, March 1, 2005.

94   **"I don't really take":** Edna Gundersen, "For Prince, It's Good to Be King," *USA Today*, June 23, 2004.

95   **"Treating your audience":** Xeni Jarden, "Music Is Not a Loaf of Bread," *Wired*, November 15, 2004.

95   **"I don't think they":** Roger McGuinn, personal interview, November 17, 2004.

97   **"The change to 'customer-*managed* relationships'":** Tom Boyles, personal interview, May 10, 2007.

99   **Everybody talks about:** Louise Story, "The High Price of Creating Free Ads," *New York Times*, May 26, 2007.

101   **"I definitely have heard that critique":** Lisa Baird, personal interview, December 1, 2007.

102 **"The JetBlue brand identity"**: Andrea Spiegel, personal interview, June 22, 2007.

103 **"Fundamentally, the consumer should have"**: Joe Tripodi, personal interview, June 19, 2007.

103 **"Visa recently embarked on a mobile"**: Kellie Krug, personal interview, June 18, 2007.

104 **"It's a very ironic question that"**: Zain Raj, personal interview, June 18, 2007.

CHAPTER 5: Innovation

106 **"When you're building a product"**: Steve Wozniak, personal interview, January 18, 2007.

109 **Robert hopes to continue:** Carol Hymowitz, "How John Deere Cut Clear Path Across Rough Field," *Wall Street Journal*, July 10, 2006.

111 **"In terms of innovation"**: Lisa Baird, *The Hub*, January-February 2007.

111 **"I actually have a concern about"**: Stephen Berkov, interview.

111 **Writing in the January 2007:** Peter Temes, "The Innovation Index," *The Hub*, January 7, 2008.

112 **As noted by Cynthia:** Cynthia Crossen, *Wall Street Journal*, May 21, 2007.

113 **In fact, over the past:** Anne Fischer, "Ideas Made Here," *Fortune*, June 12, 2007.

115 **As Tom Indoe:** Tom Indoe, "The Soul Brand," reveries.com, March 1, 1999.

116 **The problem, as reported:** Glenn Rifkin, "Saving Trees Is Music to Guitar Makers' Ears," *New York Times*, June 7, 2007.

117 **"It could alter people's"**: Ellen Byron, "Can Re-engineered Kleenex Cure Brand's Sniffles?" *Wall Street Journal*, January 22, 2007.

119 **Having "remained virtually"**: Elizabeth Esfahani, "How to Heat Up a Stodgy Brand," *Business 2.0*, November 14, 2006.

120 **Line extensions are a way:** Cameron Stracher, "Chip Shot Too Many," *Wall Street Journal*, November 2, 2007.

121 **Equally inexplicably:** Geoffrey Colvin, "Lafley and Immelt: In Search of Billions," *Fortune*, December 11, 2006.

122 **In a *Wall Street Journal*:** George Anders, *Wall Street Journal*, June 11, 2007.

123 **"Less is more" also:** Stephanie Kang, "Nike Gets Back to Basics, Reinventing the T-shirt," *Wall Street Journal*, April 2, 2007.

124 **Burberry's took a similar track:** Cecilie Rohwedder, *Wall Street Journal*, May 24, 2007.

125 **"In general, Colgate allows people":** James Figura, personal interview, December 20, 2006.

125 **"At Best Buy, the whole team":** Mike Linton, *The Hub*, January-February 2007.

126 **"Each person on the team needs to":** Stephen Berkov, *The Hub*, January-February 2007.

126 **"Most organizations, big and small":** Seth Godin, personal interview, December 4, 2006.

127 **When it comes to innovation:** Scott Thurm, "Managing Innovation," *Wall Street Journal*, September 24, 2007.

129 **Mario D'Amico is:** Mario D'Amico, "L'usine de Reves," reveries.com, July 1, 2002.

130 **"Our stats are through":** Dee Mc Laughlin, personal interview, November 9, 2007.

132 **Starwood Hotels combined:** Spencer E. Ante, "Starwood Hotels: Rubbing Customers the Right Way," *BusinessWeek*, October 8, 2007.

134 **"The celebration of misfits":** G. Pascal Zachary, "Genius and Misfit Aren't Synonyms, or Are They?" *New York Times*, June 3, 2007.

135 **His main point, as cited:** Adam Keiper, "The March of the Machines," *Wall Street Journal*, June 7, 2007.

CHAPTER 6: Investment

136 **"The cost-of-goods conversation":** Donna Sturgess, *The Hub*, July-August 2006.

139 **"Intelligentsia was known":** Michaele Weissman, "A Coffee Connoisseur on a Mission: Buy High and Sell High," *New York Times*, June 22, 2006.

141 **For the Hertzes:** Gwendolyn Bounds, "Start-Up Journal: Enterprise," *Wall Street Journal*, July 12, 2006.

142 **In fact, Atari's:** Seth Schiesel, "Atari Plays a Waiting Game with Test Drive Unlimited," *New York Times*, July 6, 2006.

143 **Heineken spent fifteen:** Adrienne Carter, "A Shining Light for Heineken," *BusinessWeek*, January 15, 2007.

144 **Their strategy centered:** Joann Muller and Jonathan Fahey, "Teflon Toyota," *Forbes*, July 3, 2006.

146 **Toyota may have:** Peter Gumbel, "BMW Drives Germany," *Time*, July 5, 2007.

147 **"Stew knew the big":** Fred Papp, personal interview, May 18, 2005.

149 **Gamal created a process:** Paula Kihla, "Six Sigma," *Business 2.0*, September 1, 2006.

151 **When Wall Street complained:** Kris Hudson, "Leader of the Club," *Wall Street Journal*, December 2007.

153 **As reported by:** Matthew Boyle, "Luxury Baseball: The $400 Glove," *Fortune*, August 24, 2007.

CHAPTER 7: Design

156 **As Lauren Boettcher:** Lisa Kalis, "The Hot Color for Cool Cars? Yellow!" *New York Times*, October 29, 2004.

157 **"At a lot of companies":** Karen Jones, personal interview, May 18, 2005.

158 **While the power:** Andy Johnson, "Tactile Branding Leads Us by Our Fingertip," *CTV News*, August 4, 2007.

160 **The problem, according:** Jonathan Welsh, *Wall Street Journal*, March 27, 2007.

160 **As Peter Gutmann wrote:** Peter Gutmann, *Wall Street Journal*, March 26, 2007.

162 **Driving home that point:** Mark Yost, "Well, the Cars Have Muscle," *Wall Street Journal*, August 22, 2007.

163 **In fact, the "oddballs":** Richard S. Chang, "On the Road with Ooh-La-La," *New York Times*, July 1, 2007.

164 **Volvo's old designs:** Jim Motavalli, "Vintage Volvos Earn Their Stripes (Ask the General Who Owns One)," *New York Times*, March 4, 2007.

166 **"I went back":** Phil Patton, "Stripping Down a Harley to Draw Young Riders," *New York Times*, March 18, 2007.

167 **"The hardest part probably":** Jan Thompson, personal interview, June 1, 2006.

168 **"This phenomenon, generated":** Allen Sarkin, "I Love It, It's Perfect, Now It Changes," *New York Times*, July 15, 2007.

170 **Michael Gibbert of Bocconi:** Michael Gibbert and David Mazursky, "A Recipe for Creating New Products," *Wall Street Journal*, October 27, 2007.

171 **That "everything that's":** Edward Rothstein, "Form Follows Function. Now Go Out and Cut the Grass," *New York Times*, May 15, 2006.

173 **The very same thing:** Matt Richtel and Eric. A. Taub, "In Battle of Consoles, Nintendo Gains Allies," *New York Times*, July 17, 2007.

174 **One of his bosses:** Norihiko Shirouzu, "One Man's Quest Put Honda in Jet Age," *Wall Street Journal*, June 19, 2007.

176 **Chuck Jones knew:** Bill Breen, "No Accounting for Design?" *Fast Company*, February 2007.

177 **"He believed that daydreaming":** Douglas Martin, "P. B. MacCready, 81, Inventor, Dies," *New York Times*, August 31, 2007.

CHAPTER 8: Experience

179 **Most of all, Andy's:** Ruth La Ferla, "The Selling of St. Andy," *New York Times*, October 26, 2006.

180 **Terry Teachout, writing:** Terry Teachout, "Andy Warhol, 15 Minutes and Counting," *Wall Street Journal*, August 6, 2003.

181 **Dina told me that:** Dina Howell, personal interview, February 16, 2007.

183 **Chris Hoyt, a widely:** Christ Hoyt, "Shopping for Consumers," *The Hub*, May 6, 2007.

184 **Stuart Armstrong thinks:** Stuart Armstrong, "Wayfinding Loyalty," *The Hub*, November 7, 2007.

186 **This one comes:** Steve Lohr, "Apple, a Success at Stores, Bet Big on Fifth Avenue," *New York Times*, May 19, 2006.

188 **"We think we came up with a way":** Simon Uwins, personal interview, July 13, 2007.

191 **Over a period:** John Eligon, "Dispensing Friendship with Clients' Stationery," *New York Times*, August 25, 2007.

192 **Described as "a cross":** Mike Albo, "Grand Old Apothecary, Version 2.0," *New York Times*, January 18, 2007.

194 **"For the packaged goods industry":** Lisa Klauser, personal interview, January 16, 2007.

194 **"The shopping experience should be fun":** Dee Mc Laughlin, *The Hub*, March-April 2007.

195 **"What we see is more movement":** Ed Gawronski, personal interview, February 6, 2007.

195 **"One of the biggest areas for improvement":** Laura Coblentz, personal interview, January 25, 2007.

195 **"We've only begun to scratch the surface":** Charlie Tarzian, personal interview, February 2, 2007.

196 **"Granted, it's a little":** Al Wittemen, "Path to Purchase," *The Hub*, July 7, 2007.

197 **Michael Gates Gill:** Joyce Wadler, "Life Changes, with a Latte to Go," *New York Times*, September 13, 2007.

199 **J. C. Penney's Michael:** Theresa Howard, "Retail Stores Pop Up for Limited Time Only," *USA Today*, May 27, 2004.

200 **For about the cost:** Hollie Shaw, *Financial Post*, April 18, 2007.

CHAPTER 9: Value

202 **As Scott Deaver:** Scott Deaver, "He Tries Harder," reveries.com, November 1, 2003.

205 **In fact, some car rental:** Gary Stoller, "Car Rental Prices Can Change in a Heartbeat," *USA Today*, March 13, 2007.

207 **According to a:** Nick Bunkley, "2 G.M. Brands, a Similar Car, but Very Different Results," *New York Times*, August 23, 2007.

209 **Tata's goal, according:** Robyn Meredith, "The Next People's Car," *Forbes*, April 16, 2007.

209 **As David Leonhardt wrote:** David Leonhardt, "Buy a Hybrid and Save a Guzzler," *New York Times,* February 8, 2006.

211 **"It is hard to be in the category":** Ann Hand, personal interview, May 30, 2007.

213 **Hal R. Varian:** Hal R. Varian, "An iPod Has Global Value. Ask the (Many) Countries That Make It," *New York Times*, June 28, 2007.

215 **"Our challenge is managing our size":** John Fleming, *The Hub*, March-April 2006.

216 **"Under the high ceilings":** David Leonhardt, "Distractions and Bargains Bought in Bulk," *New York Times*, September 13, 2006.

217 **"I always buy stuff":** Julie Bick, "24 Rolls of Toilet Paper, a Tub of Salsa and a Plasma TV," *New York Times*, January 28, 2007.

219 **"No one except us":** Julie Moskin, "For Trader Joe's, a New York Taste Test," *New York Times*, March 8, 2006.

221 **"When Disney asked":** Tom Boyles, n.p., n.d.

223 **As he told Geoffrey:** Geoffrey Colvin, "Selling P&G," *Fortune*, September 18, 2007.

CHAPTER 10: Growth

227 **After all, as Susan:** Susan Casey, "Patagonia: Blueprint for a Green Business," *Fortune*, May 29, 2007.

229 **"We manage our growth":** Rick Ridgeway, *The Hub*, January-February 2006.

230 **"The greatest key driver of growth":** Donna Sturgess, n.p., n.d.

230 **"For Dunkin' Donuts the shift":** John Gilbert, *The Hub*, January-February 2006.

231 **"Retailers should do two things":** Michael Shinall, personal interview, December 12, 2006.

232 **Google's strategy of making:** Chris Zook, "Googling Growth," *Wall Street Journal*, April 9, 2007.

234 **Hewlett-Packard, meanwhile:** Randall Stross, "A Window of Opportunity for Macs, Soon to Close," *New York Times*, September 16, 2007.

235 **Most shoppers prefer:** Mary Ellen Lloyd, "Lowe's Popularity Can't Beat Home Depot's Locations, Survey Finds," *Wall Street Journal*, April 9, 2007.

236 **As reported by:** Janet Adamy, "At Starbucks, Coffee Comes with New Décor," *Wall Street Journal,* November 10, 2006.

238 **The staple of growth:** Michael Myser, "The Staples Turnaround: That Was Easy," *Business 2.0*, June 7, 2006.

239 **Compared to the 911 Turbo:** Robert H. Frank, "The More We Make, the Better We Want," *New York Times*, September 28, 2006.

240 **As he told:** Coeli Carr, "Thank You for Insulting Our Sandals," *New York Times*, March 12, 2006.

240 **By cutting both:** Andrew Martin, "T.G.I. Friday's Finds Smaller Portions Add to Customer Traffic," *New York Times*, June 21, 2007.

240 **By keeping its factories:** Timothy Aeppel, "All About Bobcat," *Wall Street Journal*, January 1, 2007.

241 **Virgin Atlantic may have:** Daniel Michaels, *Wall Street Journal*, July 30, 2007.

243 **Rolls got there:** "Rolls-Royce at Your Service," *BusinessWeek*, November 14, 2005.

243 **According to an article:** Al Ehrbar, "Breakaway Brands," *Fortune*, October 31, 2005.

244 **As reported by Gwendolyn:** Gwendolyn Bounds, "Mr. Happy Crack Now Lures T-shirt Buyers," *Wall Street Journal*, October 25, 2005.

246 **"Our goal at Patagonia is to synchronize":** Rick Ridgeway, *The Hub*, January-February 2006.

246 **"Where in the past we drove a lot":** Donna Sturgess, n.p., n.d.

247 **"There will still be a need for classic":** John Gilbert, *The Hub*, January-February 2006.

247 **"We've seen organizations succeed":** Michael Shinall, *The Hub*, January-February 2006.

248 **Its burritos might cost:** Janet Adamy, "Chipotle's Counterintuitive Ways Wrap Up Success," *Wall Street Journal*, November 24, 2007.

250 **"If Wal-Mart does":** Casey, "Patagonia: Blueprint for a Green Business."

Index